Four Seasons

FOUR
SEASONS

An Anthology

CHOSEN BY

EDWARD PHELPS

AND

GEOFFREY SUMMERFIELD

Oxford Melbourne

OXFORD UNIVERSITY PRESS

1983

Oxford University Press, Walton Street, Oxford OX2 6DP

London Glasgow New York Toronto
Delhi Bombay Calcutta Madras Karachi
Kuala Lumpur Singapore Hong Kong Tokyo
Nairobi Dar es Salaam Cape Town
Melbourne Auckland

and associate companies in
Beirut Berlin Ibadan Mexico City Nicosia

Oxford is a trade mark of Oxford University Press

Introduction, editorial matter, and selection
© Edward Phelps and Geoffrey Summerfield 1983

British Library Cataloguing in Publication Data

Four Seasons.
1. Seasons—Literary collections
2. English literature
I. Phelps, Edward II. Summerfield, Geoffrey
820'.8'033 PR1111.S4
ISBN 0-19-212979-1

Photoset by Rowland Phototypesetting Ltd.
Bury St Edmunds, Suffolk
Printed in Great Britain by
Thomson Litho Ltd.
East Kilbride, Scotland

CONTENTS

ILLUSTRATIONS

ROBERT GIBBINGS
Title-page, and pages 22, 45, 97. Reprinted by
permission of J. M. Dent and Sons from *Sweet Thames
Run Softly*.

JOHN NASH
'Selborne Hanger', p. 29. From *The Natural History of
Selborne* by Gilbert White (The Limited Editions
Club).
'July', p. 61; 'October', p. 131; 'January', p. 193.
Reprinted by permission of The Bodley Head from
Almanack of Hope by John Pudney.
'The Farmhouse Window', p. 155. Reproduced by
permission of Crittall Windows Ltd.
The publishers gratefully acknowledge the assistance of
Mr David Wolfers, John Nash's Artistic Trustee.

GWEN RAVERAT
'April', p. 15; 'Back of the Farm', p. 57; 'The Wild
Swans', p. 107; 'Apple Pickers', p. 121; 'February',
p. 145; 'Hedgetrimming', p. 171. Reprinted by
permission of Faber and Faber Ltd. from *The Wood
Engravings of Gwen Raverat*.

ERIC RAVILIOUS
Pages 31, 41, 42, 52, 66, 70, 93, 104, 113, 116, 133, 156.
Reprinted from *Notebook and Diary* (The Kynoch Press),
and reproduced by permission of the Trustees.

C. F. TUNNICLIFFE
Pages 13, 71, 78, 177, 180, 201. Reprinted by permission
of Faber and Faber Ltd. from *The Country Child* by
Alison Uttley, illustrated by C. F. Tunnicliffe.

INTRODUCTION

Almost all of the documents in this collection were written between 50° and 60° N., in the northern temperate zone, and most were written on the eastern side of the Atlantic. For these reasons, these images and stories of the seasons will be immediately recognizable to the reader who enjoys the mixed blessings of living in such a zone.

The literature of the British Isles is rich in its record of the vagaries of the year's cycle, and in its responsiveness to the uncertain unpredictable moods of the seasons' weathers. From our early years it seems that our moods are peculiarly sensitive to light and shade, to mild breeze and chilly blast, to sunshine and cloud; it is for such an obvious reason—and perhaps for deeper philosophical reasons—that writings about the seasons have always offered two complementary and indivisible aspects, have offered indeed a sense of deep symbiosis. Talk of the elements is, willy-nilly, talk about our own inner moods; conversely, representations of our moods are mirror-images of the wayward and teasing behaviour of the elements. The pattern is one of a pre-conscious interaction.

This is not to suggest that there is any clear consensus; those who welcome the winter for the way it serves to promote sociable chat round a blazing fire—such folk are incomprehensible to those who meet the onset of winter with gritted teeth, averted gaze, or flight. Similarly, there are those who find the spring distinctively poignant, and others who resonate with extraordinary plangency to the elegiac undertones of autumn. It is presumably for such reasons that the literature of the English weather is remarkably various, rich, and eloquent.

Some commentators have decried the 'English' preoccupation with the elements, the way in which our conversations so often begin with the weather, and indeed often risk no further: but this is, we suspect, misguided. We talk of the season's weather because it is an accepted and acceptable way of allowing us to talk, however obliquely—manipulating our metaphors—about ourselves. And in the process we can of course actually talk about the weather itself. The hidden aesthete, the surreptitious artist, the reflective philosopher lurking inside the average person, has found various expressive outlets:

impressionistic gardens, abstract expressionist house-painting, connoisseurs of whiteness and greenness pretending to watch cricket, and the meditative solitaries sitting deep in thought near a fishing-rod. Such aspiring to larger, more significant, more satisfying experience and its utterance—this is also present, in a characteristically cryptic fashion, in talk of weather, of the conduct of clouds, of the brilliance or absence of the sun. Beckett, of all contemporary writers, knows this best: so, in *All That Fall*, the ostensibly innocent weather-question —'Will it hold up?'—assumes cosmic proportions before he is through; we slowly realize that the question refers to the whole confounded scheme of things!

Responsive sensibilities are not the exclusive possession of those we call artists or poets; it is the hope that this volume will reach out to the individual reader and arouse a *frisson* of recognition—it is in such a hope that we have made it. May each year be, in Edward Thomas's words, 'something that never becomes a matter of course'.

E. P. & G. S.

Four seasons fill the measure of the year;
    There are four seasons in the mind of man:
He has his lusty Spring, when fancy clear
    Takes in all beauty with an easy span:
He has his Summer, when luxuriously
    Spring's honey'd cud of youthful thought he loves
To ruminate, and by such a dreaming high
    Is nearest unto heaven: quiet coves
His soul has in its Autumn, when his wings
    He furleth close; contented so to look
On mists in idleness—to let fair things
    Pass by unheeded as a threshold brook.
He has his Winter too of pale misfeature,
Or else he would forego his mortal nature.

John Keats

The Seasons and Ourselves

EPIGRAM, proverb, joke, riddle, story, anecdote, poem, grumbling, exclamation of delight, wintry Lear on the wintry heath—all these go to make up the various means whereby we find expression for our sense of what the year and its seasons hold for us. But we not only talk about the seasons; we also talk about such talk: even, occasionally, talk about such talk about such talk!

Just as one moment moves imperceptibly into the next, with the invisible flux of time, so our moods shade subtly, one into another. But it is impossible always to register such minute gradations: we must needs impose a larger order on the confusing buzz and whirl of phenomena, both external and internal. So, just as we talk of cheerfulness, depression, elation, and melancholy, we also talk of summer, winter, spring, and autumn; and the year, like each of us, can contain them all. The 'meanings' of the seasons are our meanings.

ꟷ ꟷ ꟷ

Our seasons in the British Isles are only slightly accentuated, so that all through the year there are days which might belong to any month.

Gordon Manley, *Climate and the British Scene*, 1952

The Twelve Months

Snowy, Flowy, Blowy,
Showery, Flowery, Bowery,
Hoppy, Croppy, Droppy,
Breezy, Sneezy, Freezy.

Anon.

♣ Change of weather is the discourse of fools.

I

It is commonly observed, that when two Englishmen meet, their first talk is of the weather; they are in haste to tell each other what each must already know, that it is hot or cold, bright or cloudy, windy or calm.

Samuel Johnson, *The Idler*, June 1758

The weather was better then, or else time is stretched in fine weather, and summer evenings and red-gold skies seemed to go on till midnight, and all the doors were left wide open, to let the breezes in.

Edna O'Brien, *Mother Ireland*, 1976
[Writing of the 1940s in the 1970s.]

I think the sun's going out.

John Ruskin, *Dilecta*, 1886

Nostalgia

As one goes on
It becomes increasingly dark,
The summers are darker-leafed,
The springs rain-clouded,
The days and nights lie closer together,
The years are swept away like husks.
It is raining everywhere.

When the sun shines it is like a ghost returning,
Everywhere there are umbrellas;
Nobody heeds that pale recollection
Gliding over their heads.

In the days of my youth it came as an enchanter,
Everybody threw their hats into the sky,
The flowers burst into colour
The hills rose billowing in green pavilions
The streams ran glittering crystal
The birds carolled gambolling in the air!

I pull my hat over my eyes
The rain is come for ever
For ever and ever.

> W. J. Turner, *The Seven Days of the Sun*, 1929

In those days, I think it never rained but when one wanted it to, (and not always then).

> John Ruskin, *Praeterita*, 1885–9 [Writing of the 1840s in the 1880s.]

The poets have numbered among the felicities of the golden age, an exemption from the change of the seasons, and a perpetuity of spring; but I am not certain that in this state of imaginary happiness they have made sufficient provision for that insatiable demand of new gratifications, which seems to characterize the nature of man.

> Samuel Johnson, *The Rambler*, December 1750

If the art of flying were brought to perfection, I would follow the sun round the world, and pursue the spring through every sign of the Zodiac.

> Thomas Tickell, 1713

In verse, things are seldom said plainly and simply, as one would say them in prose; but they are described and embellished; as, for example, what you hear the watchman say often in three words, 'A cloudy morning', is said thus in verse:

> 'The dawn is overcast, the morning lowers,
> And heavily in clouds brings on the day.'

> Lord Chesterfield, *Letters to his Son*, 26 October 1739

Winds make weather; weather
Is what nasty people are
Nasty about and the nice

Show a common joy in observing:
    When I seek an image
For our Authentic City
    (Across what brigs of dread,
Down what gloomy galleries,
    Must we stagger or crawl
Before we may cry—O look!?),
    I see old men in hall-ways
Tapping their barometers,
    Or a lawn over which
The first thing after breakfast,
    A paterfamilias
Hurries to inspect his rain-gauge.

W. H. Auden, from 'Winds', *The Shield of Achilles*, 1955

Season inherits legally from dying season

W. H. Auden, 'Commentary', *In Time of War*, 1939

As sure as what is most sure,   sure as that spring primroses
Shall new-dapple next year,   sure as to-morrow morning,
Amongst come-back-again things,   things with a revival,
    things with a recovery . . .

Gerard Manley Hopkins, from 'St Winefred's Well', 1879–81

The Wheel

Through winter-time we call on spring,
And through the spring on summer call,
And when abounding hedges ring
Declare that winter's best of all;
And after that there's nothing good
Because the spring-time has not come—
Nor know that what disturbs our blood
Is but its longing for the tomb.

W. B. Yeats, *The Tower*, 1928

[*The Seasons as a Legacy of the Fall*]

>   . . . the passions all
> Have burst their bounds; and reason half extinct,
> Or impotent, or else approving, sees
> The foul disorder. Senseless, and deform'd,
> Convulsive anger storms at large; or pale,
> And silent, settles into fell revenge.
> Base envy withers at another's joy,
> And hates that excellence it cannot reach.
> Desponding fear, of feeble fancies full,
> Weak and unmanly, loosens every power.
> Ev'n love itself is bitterness of soul,
> A pensive anguish pining at the heart;
> Or, sunk to sordid interest, feels no more
> That noble wish, that never cloy'd desire,
> Which, selfish joy disdaining, seeks alone
> To bless the dearer object of its flame.
> Hope sickens with extravagance; and grief,
> Of life impatient, into madness swells;
> Or in dead silence wastes the weeping hours.
> These, and a thousand mixt emotions more,
> From ever-changing views of good and ill,
> Form'd infinitely various, vex the mind
> With endless storm; whence, deeply rankling, grows
> The partial thought, a listless unconcern,
> Cold, and averting from our neighbour's good;
> Then dark disgust, and hatred, winding wiles,
> Coward deceit, and ruffian violence:
> At last, extinct each social feeling, fell
> And joyless inhumanity pervades
> And petrifies the heart. Nature disturb'd
> Is deem'd, vindictive, to have chang'd her course.
>   Hence, in old dusky time, a deluge came:
> When the deep-cleft disparting orb, that arch'd
> The central waters round, impetuous rush'd,
> With universal burst, into the gulf,
> And o'er the high-pil'd hills of fractur'd earth

Wide dash'd the waves, in undulation vast;
Till, from the centre to the streaming clouds,
A shoreless ocean tumbled round the globe.
　　The Seasons since have, with severer sway,
Oppress'd a broken world: the Winter keen
Shook forth his waste of snows; and Summer shot
His pestilential heats. Great Spring, before,
Green all the year; and fruits and blossoms blush'd,
In social sweetness, on the self-same bough.
Pure was the temperate air; an even calm
Perpetual reign'd, save what the zephyrs bland
Breath'd o'er the blue expanse: for then nor storms
Were taught to blow, nor hurricanes to rage;
Sound slept the waters; no sulphureous glooms
Swell'd in the sky, and sent the lightning forth;
While sickly damps, and cold autumnal fogs,
Hung not, relaxing, on the springs of life.
But now, of turbid elements the sport,
From clear to cloudy tost, from hot to cold,
And dry to moist, with inward-eating change,
Our drooping days are dwindled down to nought,
Their period finish'd ere 'tis well begun.

　　　　　　　　James Thomson, from *The Seasons*, 1726–30

In the Cities

In the cities
there is even no more any weather
the weather in town is always benzine, or else petrol fumes
lubricating oil, exhaust gas.

As over some dense marsh, the fumes
thicken, miasma, the fumes of the automobile
densely thicken in the cities.

In ancient Rome, down the thronged streets
no wheels might run, no insolent chariots.

Only the footsteps, footsteps
of people
and the gentle trotting of the litter-bearers.

In Minos, in Mycenae
in all the cities with lion gates
the dead threaded the air, lingering
lingering in the earth's shadow
and leaning towards the old hearth.

In London, New York, Paris
in the bursten cities
the dead tread heavily through the muddy air
through the mire of fumes
heavily, stepping weary on our hearts.

D. H. Lawrence, Last Poems, 1932

A Child's Calendar

No visitors in January.
A snowman smokes a cold pipe in the yard.

They stand about like ancient women,
The February hills.
They have seen many a coming and going, the hills.

In March, Moorfea is littered
With knock-kneed lambs.

Daffodils at the door in April,
Three shawled Marys.
A lark splurges in galilees of sky.

And in May
A russet stallion shoulders the hill apart.
The mares tremble.

The June bee
Bumps in the pane with a heavy bag of plunder.

Strangers swarm in July
With cameras, binoculars, bird books.

He thumped the crag in August,
A blind blue whale.

September crofts get wrecked in blonde surges.
They struggle, the harvesters.
They drag loaf and ale-kirn into winter.

In October the fishmonger
Argues, pleads, threatens at the shore.

Nothing in November
But tinkers at the door, keening, with cans.

Some December midnight
Christ, lord, lie warm in our byre.
Here are stars, an ox, poverty enough.

> George Mackay Brown, *A Calendar of Love*, 1967

I suppose, that, taking this summer as a whole, people will not call it an appropriate time for praising the English climate. But for my part I will praise the English climate till I die—even if I die of the English climate. There is no weather so good as English weather. Nay, in a real sense there is no weather at all anywhere but in England. In France you have much sun and some rain; in Italy you have hot winds and cold winds; in Scotland and Ireland you have rain, either thick or thin; in America you have hells of heat and cold, and in the Tropics you have sunstrokes varied by thunderbolts. But all these you have on a broad and brutal scale, and you settle down into contentment or despair. Only in our own romantic country do you have the strictly romantic thing called Weather; beautiful and changing as a woman. The great English landscape painters (neglected now like everything that is English) have this salient distinction: that the Weather is not the atmosphere of their pictures; it is the subject of their pictures. They paint portraits of the Weather. The Weather sat to Constable. The Weather posed for Turner; and a deuce of a pose it was. This cannot truly be said of the greatest of their continental models or rivals. Poussin and Claude painted objects, ancient cities or perfect Arcadian shepherds through a clear medium of the climate. But in the English painters Weather is the hero; with Turner an Adelphi hero, taunting, flashing and fighting, melodramatic but really magnificent. The English climate, a tall and terrible protagonist, robed in rain and thunder and snow and sunlight, fills the whole canvas and the whole foreground. I admit the superiority of many other French things besides French art. But I will not yield an inch on the superiority of English weather and weather-painting. Why, the French have not even got a word for Weather; and you must ask for the weather in French as if you were asking for the time in English.

Then, again, variety of climate should always go with stability of abode. The weather in the desert is monotonous; and as a natural consequence the Arabs wander about, hoping it may be different somewhere. But an Englishman's house is not only his castle; it is his fairy castle. Clouds and colours of every varied dawn and eve are perpetually touching and turning it from clay to gold, or from gold to ivory. There is a line of woodland beyond a corner of my garden which is literally different on every one of the three hundred and sixty-five days. Sometimes it seems as near as a hedge, and sometimes as far as a faint and fiery evening cloud.

G. K. Chesterton, from 'The Glory of Grey', *Alarms and Discussions*, 1910

Weather Bestiary

RAIN

The unicorn melts through his prism. Sodden hooves
Have deluged the corn with light.

WIND

A fisherman wets his finger. The eyelash
Of the gray stallion flicks his blood with cold.

SUN

A hard summer. The month I sat at the rock
One fish rose, belly up, a dead gleam.

THUNDER

Corn, lobster, fleece hotly harvested—now
That whale stranded on the blue rock!

FROST

Stiff windless flower, hearse-blossom,
Show us the brightness of blood, stars, apples.

FOG

The sun-dipped isle was suddenly a sheep
Lost and stupid, a dense wet tremulous fleece.

SNOW

Autumn, a moulted parrot, eyes with terror
This weird white cat. It drifts the rose-bush under.

George Mackay Brown, *A Calendar of Love*, 1967

England is pre-eminently a land of atmosphere. A luminous haze
permeates everywhere, softening distances, magnifying perspectives,
transfiguring familiar objects, harmonizing the accidental, making
beautiful things magical and ugly things picturesque. Road and
pavement become wet mirrors, in which the fragments of this gross
world are shattered, inverted, and transmuted into jewels, more
appealing than precious stones to the poet, because they are insubstantial and must be loved without being possessed. Mists prolong the
most sentimental and soothing of hours, the twilight, through the long
summer evenings and the whole winter's day. In these countrysides so
full of habitations and these towns so full of verdure, lamplight and
twilight cross their rays; and the passers-by, mercifully wrapped alike
in one crepuscular mantle, are reduced to unison and simplicity, as if
sketched at one stroke by the hand of a master.

English landscape, if we think only of the land and the works of man
upon it, is seldom on the grand scale. Charming, clement, and

eminently habitable, it is almost too domestic, as if only home passions and caged souls could live there. But lift the eyes for a moment above the line of roofs or of tree-tops, and there the grandeur you miss on the earth is spread gloriously before you. The spirit of the atmosphere is not compelled, like the god of pantheism, to descend in order to exist, and wholly to diffuse itself amongst earthly objects. It exists absolutely in its own person as well, and enjoys in the sky, like a true deity, its separate life and being. There the veil of Maya, the heavenly Penelope, is being woven and rent perpetually, and the winds of destiny are always charmingly defeating their apparent intentions. Here is the playground of those early nebulous gods that had the bodies of giants and the minds of children.

In England the classic spectacle of thunderbolts and rainbows appears but seldom; such contrasts are too violent and definite for these tender skies. Here the conflict between light and darkness, like all other conflicts, ends in a compromise; cataclysms are rare, but revolution is perpetual. Everything lingers on and is modified; all is luminous and all is grey.

George Santayana, *Soliloquies in England*, 1922

Enlarge my Life with Multitude of Days,
In Health, in Sickness, thus the Suppliant prays;
Hides from himself his State, and shuns to know,
That Life protracted is protracted Woe.
Time hovers o'er, impatient to destroy,
And shuts up all the Passages of Joy:
In vain their Gifts the bounteous Seasons pour,
The Fruit autumnal, and the vernal Flow'r,
With listless Eyes the Dotard views the Store,
He views, and wonders that they please no more . . .

Samuel Johnson, from 'The Vanity of Human Wishes', 1749

All afternoon the great fleets of slow-moving summer cumulus were coming up out of the south-west, solid and intricately moulded, touched in places with a hot coppery burnish, gravely pacing the immensity of the steppe. Sergei lay in the long grass and watched them, thinking about Anton Fyodorovich's house in Ryazan Province. . . .

That's how one of my great unwritten novels starts. Another begins:—

The fog crept among the houses and patrolled the streets, like the spies and pickets of an occupying army. All the sounds of the city were muted by its grey presence. Familiar landmarks loomed strange and menacing as one walked about, as if no old loyalty could be taken for granted under the new dispensation. Somewhere out in the great grey limbo in one of the open squares, Van der Velde caught the raw wetness of the air in his throat, and coughed. 'Damn this fog,' he said. . . .

And another:—

Just before noon a fine, warm, soaking rain began to fall, turning the dusty grey slates on the roof of the church a glossy black, and whispering monotonously in the topmost branches of the elms. The rain covered Mrs Morton-Wise's spectacles with a film of fine droplets, making it increasingly difficult for her to see from where she stood what was happening on the other side of the churchyard. . . .

That's how they start, and that's how they stop. I'm all right on the measured periods describing the weather. It's the entry of Sergei, Van der Velde, Mrs Morton-Wise, and the rest, that puts the curse on them.

Who are all these people, anyway? I'm not sure that I'm terribly interested. If Van der Velde's not fat he's thin, if he hasn't got good digestion he's got bad digestion. All right, let's say he's thin with bad digestion. He hates his father, say; he marries a depressive heiress who deceives him with an art dealer; he's accused of suppressing the truth about conditions in a desiccated coconut factory. I don't know. Maybe he writes a novel about a fat man with good digestion who runs off with the wife of a schizoid bicycle designer. . . . So what? How çan I write fine prose about people's digestive troubles and bicycle designers' wives?

The weather—that's what I want to write about. What immensely evocative stuff weather is! Whenever I look out of the window and observe the meteorological condition of the day I can feel the grand periods pulsing in the blood, the nostalgic phrases ringing in my head. Whenever I look at the typewriter and see a blank piece of paper, the thin Atlantic cloud-wrack starts to scud across it immediately.

Michael Frayn, *At Bay in Gear Street*, 1967

The crocuses and the larch turning green every year a week before the others and the pastures red with uneaten sheep's placentas and the long summer days and the new-mown hay and the wood-pigeon in the morning and the cuckoo in the afternoon and the corncrake in the evening and the wasps in the jam and the smell of the gorse and the look of the gorse and the apples falling and the children walking in the dead leaves and the larch turning brown a week before the others and the chestnuts falling and the howling winds and the sea breaking over the pier and the first fires and the hooves on the road and the consumptive postman whistling 'The Roses Are Blooming in Picardy' and the standard oil-lamp and of course the snow and to be sure the sleet and bless your heart the slush and every fourth year the February débâcle and the endless April showers and the crocuses and then the whole bloody business starting all over again.

Samuel Beckett, *Watt*, 1976

SPRING

ASTRONOMICALLY, spring is the period from the spring equinox, when the night and day are equal in length—about 21 March—to the summer solstice, about 21 June. In common parlance, or according to the conventional wisdom, it is felt to extend from March to May. Etymologically, its name relates directly to the fact that it is the season when plants spring from the earth.

In the literature and traditions of the northern temperate zone, it figures as the season of renewal, revitalization, and of Eros, after the relative torpor of winter. It is certainly the season when many of us rediscover the delights of the natural world after the wearisomeness of melting snows and floods, and the latent sense of physical and spiritual attrition that descends on us towards the end of winter. The springing resurgence of life in the natural world—the boisterousness of wind, the sally of clouds, the bursting of buds—all this we have come to internalize to such a degree that we ourselves experience a sense of resurgence that can be quite disconcerting in its intensity and energy.

March said to Averil:
'I see three hoggs on yonder hill;
And if you'll lend me dayis three,
I'll find a way to gar them die!'
The first o' them was wind and weet;
The second o' them was snaw and sleet;
The third o' them was sic a freeze,
It froze the birds' feet to the trees.
When the three days were past and gane,
The silly poor hoggs came hirpling hame.

Anon.

♣ March borrows of April
  Three days, and they be ill;
  April borrows of March again
  Three days of wind and rain.

As the day goes on, the effect of tranquillity and softness lessens, and a feeling of wildness, increasing rapidly as the light dies, begins to take its place. The silence is still there, but the deadness has gone. There is life in it, a wild feeling of desolation. The air is alive with frost. Little sudden ground winds spring up with the twilight, and in the half-light the land is more than ever a white wilderness, a bitter desert of frozen drifts and dark spaces from which the snow-dust has been driven. On the cornland and the colourless empty land broken up in readiness for spring sowing, where the snow is thinnest, a mere dust of whitest ice clinging to the dark clots of earth and the wind-flattened cornshoots, dark prostrate steeples and balloons of snowless earth stretch out like shadows across the fields wherever trees have broken the force of the wind and have kept the snow from the land.

The lovely white morning snow-stillness and snow-light have gone. In their place there is a desolation of wind and cloud and frost and suddenly upscattered snow, an altogether new element of wildness and bleakness, wonderful and invigorating. The old premature spring lassitude and melancholy have gone, too. The snow has transformed everything. The half spring-like colours of the green land and the warm red trees have been covered or washed out, the fields turned to white pastures, the branches of trees bearing nothing but snow-leaves and snow-buds, the hedges covered with a light spreading of snow that is like a delicate blossoming of false blackthorn.

In the day time it was the little things that gave delight: the leaves of primrose and violet and the transparent lemon cups of winter aconite embalmed in crystal, the dead seed-plumes of grass and flowers transformed to little trees of silver, the tender blue of the snow shadows, the lace-patterns of birds' feet, the whole transfiguration of leaf and twig and stone and earth. In the twilight they have no significance. The little things are blotted out, the world is wilder and altogether grander. The tearing passage of dark cloud against the orange sunset is desolate and strange and powerful. The orange light that falls on the snow and the snowy branches and the torn edges of cloud is almost savage. The snow gleams softly orange and then pink as the west changes its light, and then blue and dark as though with smoke when the light dies at last.

And there is also no longer an absence of life or movement or sound. Starlings fly constantly over in low and disordered flocks, dipping and fetting and straggling with evening fear, the multitudinous dark underwings turned briefly orange or pink by the wild sunset light, the crescendo of the flight startling in the silence. And on the cornland or ploughed land a hare will come out and lope along and pause and huddle dark against the snow, and watch the light, and then limp on again, stopping and huddling and watching until lost beyond a ridge of land at last. And in the woods there is a constant settling and unsettling of wings and feet on frozen twigs and leaves, the pheasants croaking mournfully and beating the air with frantic flacking wings, the unseen and unknown little birds fluttering in half-terror at the night and the snow.

And in the west, above the savage orange pinkish light, the first stars are more brilliant than frost against the mass of travelling cloud. The twilight under snow is of surprising length, and the first stars seem to prolong it, shining like fierce gold flowers in the wastes of sky. And then, as the twilight lessens, the shining of the stars in the darkness above the snow creates the ultimate effect of loveliness. It brings about an effect of eternity: of eternal star-light and snow-light shining for ever.

H. E. Bates, *Through the Woods*, 1969

Thaw

Over the land freckled with snow half-thawed
The speculating rooks at their nests cawed
And saw from elm-tops, delicate as flower of grass,
What we below could not see, Winter pass.

Edward Thomas, 1916

For lo, the winter is past, the rain is over and gone; The flowers
appear on the earth; the time of the singing of birds is come, and the
voice of the turtle-dove is heard in our land.

Song of Solomon 2: 11–12

It was now the beginning of spring, the snow melting, the earth
uncovering herself, and the grass growing green, when the other
shepherds drove out their flocks to pasture, and Chloe and Daphnis
before the rest, as being servants to a greater shepherd. And forthwith
they took their course up to the Nymphs and that cave, and thence to
Pan and his pine; afterwards to their own oak, where they sat down to
look to their flocks and kiss each other. They sought about for flowers
too to crown the statues of the Gods. The soft breath of Zephyrus, and
the warm Sun, had but now brought them forth; but there were then
to be found the violet, the daffodil, the anagall [pimpernel], with the
other primes and dawnings of the spring. And when they had crowned
the statues of the Gods with them, they made a libation with new milk,
Chloe from the sheep and Daphnis from the goats. They paid too the
first-fruits of the pipe, as it were to provoke and challenge the
nightingales with their music and song. The nightingales answered
softly from the groves, and as if they remembered their long inter-
mitted song, began by little and little to jug and warble their Tereus
and Itys again.

Longus, *Daphnis and Chloe*, *c*.2nd century AD

♣ Marry in April when you can,
Joy for maiden and for man.

I had a good [blow,] and that on the high road—the very high road—on the top of the cliffs, where I met the stage-coach with all the outsides holding their hats on and themselves too, and overtook a flock of sheep with the wool about their necks blown into such great ruffs that they looked like fleecy owls. The wind played upon the light-house as if it were a great whistle, the spray was driven over the sea in a cloud of haze, the ships rolled and pitched heavily, and at intervals long slants and flaws of light made mountain-steeps of communication between the ocean and the sky. A walk of ten miles brought me to a seaside town without a cliff, which, like the town I had come from, was out of the season too. Half of the houses were shut up; half of the other half were to let; the town might have done as much business as it was doing then, if it had been at the bottom of the sea. Nobody seemed to flourish save the attorney; his clerk's pen was going in the bow-window of his wooden house; his brass doorplate alone was free from salt, and had been polished up that morning. On the beach, among the rough luggers and capstans, groups of storm-beaten boatmen, like a sort of marine monsters, watched under the lee of those objects, or stood leaning forward against the wind, looking out through battered spy-glasses. . . .

All the houses and lodgings ever let to visitors were to let that morning. It seemed to have snowed bills with To Let upon them. This put me upon thinking what the owners of all those apartments did, out of the season; how they employed their time, and occupied their minds. They could not be always going to the Methodist chapels, of which I passed one every other minute. They must have some other recreation. Whether they pretended to take one another's lodgings, and opened one another's tea-caddies in fun? Whether they cut slices off their own beef and mutton, and made believe that it belonged to somebody else? Whether they played little dramas of life, as children do, and said, 'I ought to come and look at your apartments, and you ought to ask two guineas a-week too much, and then I ought to say I must have the rest of the day to think of it, and then you ought to say that another lady and gentleman with no children in family had made an offer very close to your own terms, and you had passed your word to give them a positive answer in half an hour, and indeed were just going to take the bill down when you heard the knock, and then I ought to take them you know?' Twenty such speculations engaged my thoughts. Then, after passing, still clinging to the walls, defaced rags of the bills of last year's Circus, I came to a back field near a timber-yard where the Circus itself had been, and where there was yet a sort of monkish tonsure on the grass, indicating the spot where the young lady had gone round upon her pet steed Firefly in her daring flight. Turning into the town again, I came among the shops, and they were emphatically out of the season. The chemist had no boxes of ginger-beer powders, no beautifying sea-side soaps and washes, no attractive scents; nothing but his great goggle-eyed red bottles, looking as if the winds of winter and the drift of the salt sea had inflamed them. The grocers' hot pickles, Harvey's Sauce, Doctor Kitchener's Zest, Anchovy Paste, Dundee Marmalade, and the whole stock of luxurious helps to appetite, were hibernating somewhere underground. The china-shop had no trifles from anywhere. The Bazaar had given in altogether, and presented a notice on the shutters that this establishment would re-open at Whitsuntide, and that the proprietor in the meantime might be heard of at Wild Lodge, East Cliff. At the Sea-bathing Establishment, a row of neat little wooden houses seven or eight feet high, I *saw* the proprietor in bed in the shower-bath. As to the bathing machines, they were (how they got there is not for me to say) at the top of a hill at least a mile and a half off.

Charles Dickens, 'Out of the Season', *Reprinted Pieces*, 1868

Now fades the last long streak of snow,
    Now burgeons every maze of quick
    About the flowering squares, and thick
By ashen roots the violets blow.

Now rings the woodland loud and long,
    The distance takes a lovelier hue,
    And drown'd in yonder living blue
The lark becomes a sightless song.

Now dance the lights on lawn and lea,
    The flocks are whiter down the vale,
    And milkier every milky sail
On winding stream or distant sea;

Where now the seamew pipes, or dives
    In yonder greening gleam, and fly
    The happy birds, that change their sky
To build and brood; that live their lives

From land to land; and in my breast
    Spring wakens too; and my regret
    Becomes an April violet,
And buds and blossoms like the rest.

                Alfred, Lord Tennyson, from 'In Memoriam', 1850

♣ A cold April the barn will fill.

First sight of Spring

The hazel blooms in threads of crimson hue
Peep through the swelling buds and look for spring
Ere yet a white thorn leaf appears in view
Or march finds throstles pleased enough to sing
On the old touchwood tree wood peckers cling
A moment and their harsh toned notes renew
In happier mood the stockdove claps his wing
The squirrel sputters up the powdered oak
With tail cocked oer his head and ears errect
Startled to hear the woodmans understroke
And with the courage that his fears collect
He hisses fierce half malice and half glee
Leaping from branch to branch about the tree
In winters foliage moss and lichens drest

Wood Pictures in Spring

The rich brown umber hue the oaks unfold
When springs young sunshine bathes their trunks in gold
So rich so beautiful so past the power
Of words to paint—my heart aches for the dower
The pencil gives to soften and infuse
This brown luxuriance of unfolding hues

This living lus[c]ious tinting woodlands give
Into a landscape that might breath and live
And this old gate that claps against the tree
The entrance of springs paradise should be
Yet paint itself with living nature fails
—The sunshine threading through these broken rails
In mellow shades—no pencil eer conveys
And mind alone feels fancies and pourtrays

John Clare (1793–1864)

Green Stain

A filth of leaves, she said, a froth, she said
Of sudsy flowers, and there's your mawkish Spring.
Oh, barebone tree, what has it done to you?
Black field, you're gone but for remembering.

I keep my winter where my heart should be.
—I'd rather bear it in its blackest moods
Than see those frilly leaves and blossoms make
A haberdashery of wholesome woods.

A mish-mash green, a sickly groping, such
A fumbling into light! How could they surpass
The icy shapes of darling winter hidden
In luckless trees and ill-starred meadow grass?

Norman MacCaig, *A Man In My Position*, 1969

The first joy of the year being in its snowdrops, the second, and cardinal one, was in the almond blossom,—every other garden and woodland gladness following from that in an unbroken order of kindling flower and shadowy leaf; and for many and many a year to come,—until, indeed, the whole of life became autumn to me,—my chief prayer for the kindness of heaven, in its flowerful seasons, was that the frost might not touch the almond blossom.

John Ruskin, *Praeterita*, 1885-9

Long ago the remark was made in a March issue of *Punch* that 'spring has set in with its accustomed severity'. This expression indeed was used in a letter by Coleridge written at the beginning of May in 1826; but he in turn may have known that Madame de Sévigné used a similar phrase in 1689. Adopting the division of the year into four seasons of equal length, a division likely to appeal to most meteorologists in mid-temperate latitudes, it is undoubtedly best to consider March, April and May as comprising the spring. But surrounded as we are by the sea the rise of temperature with the lengthening day is slow and frequently suffers many setbacks; hence in Britain we have a very long season during which one after another of the familiar harbingers of spring appear. Many of our flowers derive from wild ancestors with an open deciduous woodland habitat, where they quickly responded to the increased light while the trees were still bare. Hence such flowers as crocus and daffodil, anemone and bluebell successively appear to remind us of the approaching warmer season.

Gordon Manley, *Climate and the British Scene*, 1952

♣ March many weathers.

March is a rude, and sometimes boisterous month, possessing many of the characteristics of winter, yet awakening sensations perhaps more delicious than the following spring months, for it gives us the first announcement and taste of spring. What can equal the delight of our hearts at the very first glimpse of spring—the first springing of buds and green herbs. It is like a new life infused into our bosoms. A spirit of tenderness, a burst of freshness and luxury of feeling possesses us:

and let fifty springs have broken upon us, *this* joy, unlike many joys of time, is not an atom impaired. Are we not young? Are we not boys? Do we not break, by the power of awakened thoughts, into all the rapturous scenes of all our happier years? There is something in the freshness of the soil—in the mossy bank—the balmy air—the voices of birds—the early and delicious flowers, that we have seen and felt *only* in *childhood* and *spring*.

William Howitt, *Book of the Seasons*, 1833

Spring

1. Goldfish.
2. White mice.
3. Carrot tops. Twigs in earth.
4. Types of birds. Birds' footprints.
5. Feeding the birds.
6. Growth stages of bulbs and tree seedlings.
7. Green and not-green parts of a plant.
8. Clouds, points of compass, pole star.
9. Catkins and early spring flowers.
10. Zoo animals.
11. Frog spawn.
12. Farm animals.
13. Farm poultry.
14. Bark patterns.
15. Nocturnal animals and birds.

E. M. Stephenson, *Nature Study and Rural Science*,
A Four Year Course for Juniors, 1966

The phenomena of the year take place every day in a pond on a small scale. Every morning, generally speaking, the shallow water is being warmed more rapidly than the deep, though it may not be made so warm after all, and every evening it is being cooled more rapidly until the morning. The day is an epitome of the year. The night is the winter, the morning and evening are the spring and fall, and the noon is the summer. The crackling and booming of the ice indicate a change of temperature. One pleasant morning after a cold night, 24th February 1850, having gone to Flint's Pond to spend the day, I noticed with surprise, that when I struck the ice with the head of my axe, it resounded like a gong for many rods around, or as if I had struck on a tight drum-head. The pond began to boom about an hour after sunrise, when it felt the influence of the sun's rays slanted upon it from over the hills; it stretched itself and yawned like a waking man with a gradually increasing tumult, which was kept up three or four hours. It took a short siesta at noon, and boomed once more toward night, as the sun was withdrawing his influence. In the right stage of the weather a pond fires its evening gun with great regularity. But in the middle of the day, being full of cracks, and the air also less elastic, it had completely lost its resonance, and probably fishes and musk-rats could not then have been stunned by a blow on it. The fishermen say that the 'thundering of the pond' scares the fishes and prevents their biting. The pond does not thunder every evening, and I cannot tell surely when to expect its thundering; but though I may perceive no difference in the weather, it does. Who would have expected so large and cold and thick-skinned a thing to be so sensitive? Yet it has its law to which it thunders obedience when it should as surely as the buds expand in the spring. The earth is all alive and covered with papillæ. The largest pond is as sensitive to atmospheric changes as the globule of mercury in its tube.

Henry Thoreau, *Walden*, 1854

When spring came, after that hard winter, one could not get enough of the nimble air. Every morning I wakened with a fresh consciousness that winter was over. There were none of the signs of spring for which I used to watch in Virginia, no budding woods or blooming gardens. There was only—spring itself; the throb of it, the light restlessness, the vital essence of it everywhere: in the sky, in the swift clouds, in the pale sunshine, and in the warm, high wind—rising suddenly, sinking suddenly, impulsive and playful like a big puppy that pawed you and then lay down to be petted. If I had been tossed down blindfold on that red prairie, I should have known that it was spring.

Everywhere now there was the smell of burning grass. Our neighbours burned off their pasture before the new grass made a start, so that the fresh growth would not be mixed with the dead stand of last year. Those light, swift fires, running about the country, seemed a part of the same kindling that was in the air.

Willa Cather, My Ántonia, 1918

Though (by statute 4 and 5 W. and Mary, c. 23) 'to burn on any waste, between Candlemas and Midsummer, any grig, ling, heath and furze, goss or fern, is punishable with whipping and confinement in the house of correction'; yet, in this forest, about March or April, according to the dryness of the season, such vast heath-fires are lighted up, that they often get to a masterless head, and, catching the hedges, have sometimes been communicated to the underwoods, woods, and coppices, where great damage has ensued. The plea for these burnings is, that, when the old coat of heath, etc., is consumed, young will sprout up, and afford much tender browse for cattle; but, where there is large old furze, the fire, following the roots, consumes the very ground; so that for hundreds of acres nothing is to be seen but smother and desolation, the whole circuit round looking like the cinders of a volcano; and the soil being quite exhausted, no traces of vegetation are to be found for years. These conflagrations, as they take place usually with a north-east or east wind, much annoy this village with their smoke, and often alarm the country; and, once in particular, I remember that a gentleman, who lives beyond Andover, coming to my house, when he got on the downs between that town and Winchester, at twenty-five miles distance, was surprised much with smoke and a hot smell of fire; and concluded that Alresford was in flames; but, when he came to that town, he then had apprehensions for the next village, and so on to the end of his journey.

Gilbert White, The Natural History of Selborne, 1789

When London people walk out of town, like bees from a hive (only seldom on so good an errand), how entirely unacquainted they appear to be, with the warning which the rising clouds give of the approach of a shower. It looks strange, if not laughable, to see a number of well-dressed people, sauntering with the utmost composure from their homes, full in the face of a black and thickening cloud, which in ten minutes is to involve them in trouble and vexation.

Robert Bloomfield, 'Reflections' from The Remains, Vol. 2, 1824

♣ Though the sun shines, leave not your cloak at home.

[*March 1866*]

. . . February passed like a skate and I know March. Here is the 'light' the stranger said 'was not on sea or land.' Myself could arrest it, but will not chagrin him.

. . . Cousin Peter told me the Doctor would address Commencement—trusting it insure you both for papa's fete I endowed Peter.

We do not always know the source of the smile that flows to us. . . .

My flowers are near and foreign, and I have but to cross the floor to stand in the Spice Isles.

The wind blows gay today and the jays bark like blue terriers.

I tell you what I see—the landscape of the spirit requires a lung, but no tongue. I hold you few I love, till my heart is red as February and purple as March.

Hand for the Doctor.

Emily.

Emily Dickinson (1830–86), *Letters to the Hollands*
ed. Theodora Van Wagenen Ward, 1951

A Light exists in Spring
Not present on the Year
At any other period—
When March is scarcely here

A Colour stands abroad
On Solitary Fields
That Science cannot overtake
But Human Nature feels.

It waits upon the Lawn,
It shows the furthest Tree
Upon the furthest Slope you know
It almost speaks to you.

Then as Horizons step
Or Noons report away
Without the Formula of sound
It passes and we stay–

A quality of loss
Affecting our Content
As Trade had suddenly encroached
Upon a Sacrament.

Emily Dickinson

A silent, dim, distanceless, steaming, rotting day in March. The last brown oak-leaf which had stood out the winter's frost spun and quivered plump down, and then lay; as if ashamed to have broken for a moment the ghastly stillness, like an awkward guest at a great dumb dinner-party. A cold suck of wind just proved its existence, by toothaches on the north side of all faces. The spiders, having been weather-bewitched the night before, had unanimously agreed to cover every brake and brier with gossamer-cradles, and never a fly to be caught in them; like Manchester cotton-spinners madly glutting the markets in the teeth of 'no demand'. The steam crawled out of the dank turf, and reeked off the flanks and nostrils of the shivering horses, and clung with clammy paws to frosted hats and dripping boughs. A soulless, skyless, catarrhal day, as if that bustling dowager, old mother Earth—what with match-making in spring, and *fêtes champêtres* in summer, and dinner-giving in autumn—was fairly worn out, and put to bed with the influenza, under wet blankets and the cold-water cure.

There sat Lancelot by the cover-side, his knees aching with cold and wet, thanking his stars that he was not one of the whippers-in who were lashing about in the dripping cover . . .

But 'all things do end', and so did this; and the silence of the hounds also; . . . and Lancelot began to stalk slowly with a dozen horsemen up the wood-ride, to a fitful accompaniment of wandering hound-music, where the choristers were as invisible as nightingales among the thick cover. And hark! . . . the sweet hubbub suddenly crashed out into one jubilant shriek, and then swept away fainter and fainter among the trees. The walk became a trot—the trot a canter. Then a

faint melancholy shout at a distance, answered by a 'Stole away!' from the fields; a doleful 'toot!' of the horn; the dull thunder of many horse-hoofs rolling along the further wood-side. Then red coats, flashing like sparks of fire across the grey gap of mist at the ride's-mouth, then a whipper-in, bringing up a belated hound, burst into the pathway, smashing and plunging, with shut eyes, through ash-saplings and hassock-grass; then a fat farmer, sedulously pounding through the mud, was overtaken and bespattered in spite of all his struggles;—until the line streamed out into the wide rushy pasture, starting up pewits and curlews, as horsemen poured in from every side, and cunning old farmers rode off at inexplicable angles to some well-known haunts of pug: and right ahead, chiming and jangling sweet madness, the dappled pack glanced and wavered through the veil of soft grey mist.

Charles Kingsley, *Yeast*, 1850

♣ A windy March and a rainy April make a beautiful May.

To see the wind, with a man his eyes, it is unpossible, the nature of it is so fine, and subtle, yet this experience of the wind had I once myself, and that was in the great snow that fell four years ago: I rode in the highway betwixt Topcliffe-upon-Swale, and Borowe Bridge, the way being somewhat trodden afore, by wayfaring men. The fields on both sides were plain and lay almost yard deep with snow, the night afore had been a little frost, so that the snow was hard and crusted above. That morning the sun shone bright and clear, the wind was whistling aloft, and sharp according to the time of the year. The snow in the highway lay loose and trodden with horse feet: so as the wind blew, it took the loose snow with it, and made it so slide upon the snow in the field which was hard and crusted by reason of the frost overnight, that thereby I might see very well, the whole nature of the wind as it blew that day. And I had a great delight and pleasure to mark it, which maketh me now far better to remember it. Sometime the wind would be not past two yards broad, and so it would carry the snow as far as I could see. Another time the snow would blow over half the field at once. Sometime the snow would tumble softly, by and by it would fly wonderfull fast. And this I perceived also that the wind goeth by streams and not whole together. For I should see one stream within a score on me, then the space of two score no snow would stir, but after so much quantity of ground, another stream of snow at the same very time should be carried likewise, but not equally. For the one would stand still when the other flew apace, and so continue sometime swiftlier, sometime slowlier, sometime broader, sometime narrower, as far as I could see. Nor it flew not straight, but sometime it crooked this way sometime that way, and sometime it ran round about in a compass. And sometime the snow would be lift clean from the ground up into the air, and by and by it would be all clapped to the ground as though there had been no wind at all, straightway it would rise and fly again.

And that which was the most marvel of all, at one time two drifts of snow flew, the one out of the West into the East, the other out of the North into the East: And I saw two winds by reason of the snow the one cross over the other, as it had been two highways. And again I should hear the wind blow in the air, when nothing was stirred at the ground. And when all was still where I rode, not very far from me the snow should be lifted wonderfully. This experience made me more marvel at the nature of the wind, than it made me cunning in the knowledge of the wind: but yet thereby I learned perfectly that it is no marvel at all though men in a wind lose their length in shooting, seeing so many ways the wind is so variable in blowing.

Roger Ascham, *Toxophilus*, 1545

The masterful wind was up and out, shouting and chasing, the lord of the morning. Poplars swayed and tossed with a roaring swish; dead leaves sprang aloft, and whirled into space; and all the clear-swept heaven seemed to thrill with sound like a great harp. It was one of the first awakenings of the year. The earth stretched herself, smiling in her sleep; and everything leapt and pulsed to the stir of the giant's movement. With us it was a whole holiday; the occasion a birthday

—it matters not whose. Some one of us had had presents, and pretty conventional speeches, and had glowed with that sense of heroism which is no less sweet that nothing has been done to deserve it. But the holiday was for all, the rapture of awakening Nature for all, the various outdoor joys of puddles and sun and hedge-breaking for all. Colt-like I ran through the meadows, frisking happy heels in the face of Nature laughing responsive. Above, the sky was bluest of the blue; wide pools left by the winter's floods flashed the colour back, true and brilliant; and the soft air thrilled with the germinating touch that seems to kindle something in my own small person as well as in the rash primrose already lurking in sheltered haunts. Out into the brimming sun-bathed world I sped, free of lessons, free of discipline and correction, for one day at least. My legs ran of themselves, and though I heard my name called faint and shrill behind, there was no stopping for me. . . .

The air was wine, the moist earth-smell wine, the lark's song, the wafts from the cowshed at top of the field, the pant and smoke of a distant train—all were wine—or song, was it? Or odour, this unity they all blent into? I had no words then to describe it, that earth-effluence of which I was so conscious; nor, indeed, have I found words since. I ran sideways, shouting; I dug glad heels into the squelching soil; I splashed diamond showers from puddles with a stick; I hurled clods skywards at random, and presently I somehow found myself singing. The words were mere nonsense—irresponsible babble; the tune was an improvisation, a weary unrhythmic thing of rise and fall; and yet it seemed to me a genuine utterance, and just at that moment the one thing fitting and right and perfect. . . .

A puff on the right cheek from my wilful companion sent me off at a fresh angle, and presently I came in sight of the village church, sitting solitary within its circle of elms. From forth the vestry window projected two small legs, gyrating, hungry for foothold, with larceny —not to say sacrilege—in their every wriggle; a godless sight for a supporter of the Establishment. Though the rest was hidden, I knew the legs well enough; they were usually attached to the body of Bill Saunders, the peerless bad boy of the village. Bill's coveted booty, too, I could easily guess at that; it came from the Vicar's store of biscuits, kept (as I knew) in a cupboard along with his official trappings. For a moment I hesitated; then I passed on my way. I protest I was not on Bill's side; but then, neither was I on the Vicar's, and there was something in this immoral morning which seemed to say that perhaps, after all, Bill had as much right to the biscuits as the Vicar, and would certainly enjoy them better; and anyhow it was a disputable point, and no business of mine. Nature, who had accepted me for ally, cared little who had the world's biscuits, and assuredly was not going to let any friend of hers waste his time in playing policeman for Society.

Kenneth Grahame, *The Golden Age*, 1895

Spring

Nothing is so beautiful as Spring—
    When weeds, in wheels, shoot long and lovely and lush;
    Thrush's eggs look little low heavens, and thrush
Through the echoing timber does so rinse and wring
The ear, it strikes like lightnings to hear him sing;
    The glassy peartree leaves and blooms, they brush
    The descending blue; that blue is all in a rush
With richness; the racing lambs too have fair their fling.

What is all this juice and all this joy?
    A strain of the earth's sweet being in the beginning
In Eden garden.—Have, get, before it cloy,

    Before it cloud, Christ, lord, and sour with sinning,
Innocent mind and Mayday in girl and boy,
    Most, O maid's child, thy choice and worthy the winning.

Gerard Manley Hopkins, May 1877

♣ A bushel of March dust, on the leaves, is worth a king's ransom.

Primroses remain among the best loved of our spring flowers. Many appear before sufficient insects are abroad to pollinate them—hence Shakespeare's 'pale primroses that die unmarried'. However, their life can be extended by crystallizing the flowers, using the following ingredients:

1 saltspoon of gum tragacanth (buy this from a good chemist or health-food store)

2 tablespoons of triple-strength rose-water (which may be purchased from the same sources)

Castor sugar

Mix the gum and rose-water in a screw-top jar and leave in a warm place for 24 hours. Cut a bunch of primrose flowers, leaving sufficient stalk to hold them by, and, using a fine brush, coat each petal with the mixture. Dip the flowers in the castor sugar and leave them to dry.

Having snipped off the stems, store the primroses in a jar and use them to decorate chocolate cakes.

'Food From Your Garden', 1977

Along these blushing borders, bright with dew,
And in yon mingled wilderness of flowers,
Fair-handed Spring unbosoms every grace;
Throws out the snowdrop, and the crocus first;
The daisy, primrose, violet darkly blue,
And polyanthus of unnumber'd dyes;
The yellow wall-flower, stain'd with iron brown;
And lavish stock that scents the garden round:
From the soft wing of vernal breezes shed,
Anemonies; auriculas, enrich'd
With shining meal o'er all their velvet leaves;
And full ranunculas, of glowing red.
Then comes the tulip-race, where Beauty plays
Her idle freaks; from family diffus'd
To family, as flies the father dust,
The varied colours run; and, while they break
On the charm'd eye, th' exulting florist marks,
With secret pride, the wonders of his hand.
No gradual bloom is wanting; from the bud,
First-born of Spring, to Summer's musky tribes;
Nor hyacinths, of purest virgin white,
Low-bent, and blushing inward; nor jonquilles,
Of potent fragrance; nor narcissus fair,
As o'er the fabled fountain hanging still;
Nor broad carnations, nor gay-spotted pinks;

34

Nor, shower'd from every bush, the damask rose.
Infinite numbers, delicacies, smells,
With hues on hues expression cannot paint,
The breath of Nature, and her endless bloom.

James Thomson, from *The Seasons*, 1726–30

When daffodils begin to peer,
    With heigh! the doxy, over the dale,
Why, then comes in the sweet o' the year;
    For the red blood reigns in the winter's pale.

The white sheet bleaching on the hedge,
    With heigh! the sweet birds, O, how they sing!
Doth set my pugging tooth on edge;
    For a quart of ale is a dish for a king.

The lark, that tirra-lirra chants,
    With, heigh! with, heigh! the thrush and the jay,
Are summer songs for me and my aunts,
    While we lie tumbling in the hay.

William Shakespeare, *The Winter's Tale, c.*1623

I wandered lonely as a cloud
That floats on high o'er vales and hills,
When all at once I saw a crowd,
A host, of golden daffodils;
Beside the lake, beneath the trees,
Fluttering and dancing in the breeze.

Continuous as the stars that shine
And twinkle on the milky way,
They stretched in never-ending line
Along the margin of a bay:
Ten thousand saw I at a glance,
Tossing their heads in sprightly dance.

35

The waves beside them danced; but they
Out-did the sparkling waves in glee:
A poet could not but be gay,
In such a jocund company:
I gazed—and gazed—but little thought
What wealth the show to me had brought:

For oft, when on my couch I lie
In vacant or in pensive mood,
They flash upon that inward eye
Which is the bliss of solitude;
And then my heart with pleasure fills,
And dances with the daffodils.

William Wordsworth, 1804

Now the full-throated daffodils,
Our trumpeters in gold,
Call resurrection from the ground
And bid the year be bold.

Today the almond tree turns pink,
The first flush of the spring;
Winds loll and gossip through the town
Her secret whispering.

Now too the bird must try his voice
Upon the morning air;
Down drowsy avenues he cries
A novel great affair.

He tells of royalty to be;
How with her train of rose
Summer to coronation comes
Through waving wild hedgerows.

Today crowds quicken in a street,
The fish leaps in the flood:
Look there, gasometer rises,
And here bough swells to bud.

For our love's luck, our stowaway,
Stretches in his cabin;
Our youngster joy barely conceived
Shows up beneath the skin.

Our joy was but a gusty thing
Without sinew or wit,
An infant flyaway; but now
We make a man of it.

C. Day-Lewis, *From Feathers to Iron*, 1931

No one can deny but that the same power which brings forth the leaves of trees, will also make the grain vegetate; nor can any one assert that a premature sowing will always, and in every place, accelerate a ripe harvest. Perhaps, therefore, we cannot promise ourselves a happy success by any means so likely, as by taking our rule for sowing from the leafing of trees. We must, for that end, observe in what order every tree puts forth its leaves. To these most ingenious remarks Mr. Barck has added the order of the leafing of trees in Sweden. Mr. Stillingfleet is the only person that has made correct observations upon the foliation of the trees and shrubs of this kingdom. The following is his calendar, made in Norfolk, 1765.

1. Honeysuckle . .	Jan. 15	15. Alder	——— 7
2. Gooseberry . .	Mar. 11	16. Sycamore . . .	——— 9
3. Currant . . .	——— 11	17. Elm.	——— 10
4. Elder	——— 11	18. Quince. . . .	——— 10
5. Birch	April 1	19. Marsh Elder . .	April 11
6. Weeping Willow .	——— 1	20. Wych Elm . . .	——— 12
7. Raspberry . . .	——— 3	21. Quicken Tree . .	——— 13
8. Bramble . . .	——— 3	22. Hornbeam . . .	——— 13
9. Briar	——— 4	23. Apple Tree . .	——— 14
10. Plum	——— 6	24. Abele	——— 16
11. Apricot. . . .	——— 6	25. Chestnut . . .	——— 16
12. Peach	——— 6	26. Willow	——— 17
13. Filbert	——— 7	27. Oak	——— 18
14. Sallow	——— 7	28. Lime	——— 19

29. Maple . . . . —— 21	33. Beech . . . . . —— 21
30. Walnut . . . . —— 21	34. Acacia Robinia . —— 21
31. Plane . . . . —— 21	35. Ash . . . . . —— 22
32. Black Poplar . . —— 21	36. Carolina Poplar . —— 22

In different years, and in different soils and expositions, these trees and shrubs vary as to their leafing, but they are invariable as to their succession, being bound down to it by Nature herself: a farmer, therefore, who would use this sublime idea of Linnæus, should diligently mark the time of budding, leafing, and flowering of different plants. He should also put down the days on which his respective grains were sown; and, by comparing these two tables for a number of years, he will be enabled to form an exact calendar for his spring corn.

William Howitt, *Book of the Seasons*, 1833

[*Opal Whiteley was seven years old when she began her diary in the lumber camps of Oregon in the early 1900s*]

A beetle went across the path and a salal bush did nod itself to us. The wind made little soft whispers, and by and by we was come to the log. My friend did kneel down by it, and she looked looks for a long time at all the bunches of flowers. And I did say a little prayer and Thomas Chatterton Jupiter Zeus [a tame wood-rat] did squeak a little squeak. I made counts of the bunches of flowers, and they were thirty-and-three. I saw a chipmunk, and I followed him after to see how many stripes he did have on his back and where was his home; and on the way I saw other birds and I followed them after on tiptoes to have sees where they were having goes to. And in the bushes there was a little nest with four eggs in it with speckles on them. I did have thinks there was needs for me to pick out names for the little birds that will hatch out of those eggs. This is a very busy world to live in. There is much needs for picking out names for things.

The Diary of Opal Whiteley, 1920

♣ When April blows his horn it's good for both hay and corn.

FRIDAY 1ST APRIL
The lamb born on Tuesday died during the night and Graham has put in our only remaining orphan lamb with the ewe. He's had to tie the ewe up so that the lamb has a chance to suckle. It will be a relief not to have to make up any more bottles.

Graham and David finished fencing in Long Close where the sheep are now eating the last of the roots. Once they have finished we shall plough it up and drill barley.

SATURDAY 2ND
David spread fertiliser on Lawn Field and Burrow Meadow so the grass should come on this year. They are patchy fields both of them with overhanging oaks and elms preventing the grass from getting the sunshine it needs.

The bulk milk lorry is playing havoc with Burrow Lane, carving great furrows into the chippings. We shall have to concrete the lane at some stage, and at this rate of deterioration it will have to be soon.

SUNDAY 3RD
Graham cleaned out the pigs' house and the calves' house before lunch and fixed up the broken gate on Burrow Meadow.

A sunny Sunday with the ground drying fast all the time. It will be a week of harrowing and tilling if the weather stays right. There's a busy fortnight ahead.

John let the four big steers on to Ferny Piece to graze this afternoon and they are staying out tonight—the first night out after the winter. . . .

FRIDAY 8TH APRIL
Good Friday and hot cross buns, but with the snow and frost in the early morning it seemed more like Christmas than Easter. There are more snow showers on the way, but meanwhile the ground is dry and right for tilling. John and Graham took packed lunches and two tractors off up to Berry and drilled all day. We don't like to work on Good Friday—but John will not rest now till it's done and we have to take the opportunity while we can. There may be snow around or rain, and he wants to get the corn in.

The yield is down a little to 154 gallons—that's close on 4 gallons a cow, but the cows are eating down what little grass there is all too quickly and there will be no more growth for a while.

David winnowed another 14 cwt. of barley this afternoon; there's still another ton to do.

SATURDAY 9TH

The drilling goes on in dry weather. Both Quarry Park and Little Eastern Hill are finished now—so there is only Dutch Barn Field over at Berry still to do.

While David was down at milking, Hettie noticed a ewe in trouble on Front Meadow. The ewe had lambed only the day before yesterday and was lying quite still. Hettie saw that she had a prolapse. She rang up the vet at once who came, pushing everything back in where it should be, and stitched the ewe up again.

SUNDAY 10TH

Easter Day, and with most of the drilling now done and the rain falling all day, everyone could relax.

MONDAY 11TH

It has dried off well during the night and John and Graham were able to get out early to finish up over at Berry. They tilled and harrowed the last field. Harrowing is the last part of the process and entails pulling light drags over the field to cover up the seed. One slight hitch, John ran out of seed corn, and had to run across to George Dunn's at Brimblecombe for a bucket and a half of corn for the last few square feet. But it's all done now, and although there is a lot more ploughing, drilling and harrowing to be done close to home, the main corn crop is in and there is warmer weather forecast.

We had to fetch another load of hay from Morley King's. We are not buying it directly—we will be letting him have some of our hay back in return when it's harvested. The grass still is not growing, although the rooks are nesting and the blossoms are out everywhere.

Michael Morpurgo, *All Around the Year*, 1979

Caution in Seed-time

Nae hurry wi' your corns,
   Nae hurry wi' your harrows;
Snaw lies ahint the dike,
   Mair may come and fill the furrows.

Anon.

Sowing

It was a perfect day
For sowing; just
As sweet and dry was the ground
As tobacco-dust.

I tasted deep the hour
Between the far
Owl's chuckling first soft cry
And the first star.

A long stretched hour it was;
Nothing undone
Remained; the early seeds
All safely sown.

And now, hark at the rain,
Windless and light,
Half a kiss, half a tear,
Saying good-night.

Edward Thomas, 1915

Suburban Spring in Warwickshire
for Lilac

First then the prunus and the Japanese cherry,
fragile but assertive before the year warms up;
appropriate to this suburb, these houses

and their people, not native here,
but forcing quick colour, short-lasting,
out of a thin top-soil.

Rather I wait for the chestnut flowering
and the dripping laburnum blossoms;
for the chestnuts later will yield
the spiky fruit with the ivory kernels,
and, for small boys, the knuckled challenges:

and the pale-gilt laburnum recalls
the small tree which hung beside the fence,
where you could climb over to play
with your friends next door:
its pods I was warned against, repeatedly.
I was seven then:
it was my grandmother's garden,
in another country.

John Hewitt, *Out of My Time*, 1974

Repeat that, repeat,
Cuckoo, bird, and open ear wells, heart-springs, delightfully sweet,
With a ballad, with a ballad, a rebound
Off trundled timber and scoops of the hillside ground, hollow hollow
    hollow ground:
The whole landscape flushes on a sudden at a sound.

Gerard Manley Hopkins (1844–89)

The First Swallow

April 13: Hirundo domestica!!!

Gilbert White, *Journal*, 1768

Now the customary beautiful Easter Eve Idyll had fairly begun and people kept arriving from all parts with flowers to dress the graves. Children were coming from the town and from neighbouring villages with baskets of flowers and knives to cut holes in the turf. The roads were lively with people coming and going and the churchyard a busy scene with women and children and a few men moving about among the tombstones and kneeling down beside the green mounds flowering the graves. An evil woman from Hay was dressing a grave. (Jane Phillips). I found a child wandering about the tombs looking for her father's grave. She had found her grandfather's and had already dressed it with flowers. The clerk was banking up and watering the green mounds not far off and I got him to come and show the child where her father's grave lay. He soon found it for he knows almost every grave in the churchyard. And then I helped the child to dress the long narrow green mound with the flowers that remained in her basket, some of which came from the Cabalva greenhouse. We found two more graves of her family close by her father's, an uncle of hers and a child, a cousin or sister. The two brothers lay side by side. My little friend had lavished so much of her flower wealth upon her grandfather's grave that there was not much left for the others and we were obliged to economize and make our scanty store go as far as possible. I showed her how to arrange the flowers in the form of a cross, and she went away satisfied and happy at the result of her work. . . .

More and more people kept coming into the churchyard as they finished their day's work. The sun went down in glory behind the dingle, but still the work of love went on through the twilight and into the dusk until the moon rose full and splendid. The figures continued to move about among the graves and to bend over the green mounds in the calm clear moonlight and warm air of the balmy evening. . . .

At 8 o'clock there was a gathering of the Choir in the Church to practise the two anthems for to-morrow, and the young people came

43

flocking in from the graves where they had been at work or watching others working, or talking to their friends, for the Churchyard on Easter Eve is a place where a great many people meet. The clerk's wife had been cleaning the church for Easter Day and the clerk had kept the church jealously locked as there were so many strangers about in the churchyard. He now unlocked the steeple door and let us in that way. There was a large gathering of the Choir and two or three people stole in from the churchyard afterwards to hear the anthems practised. The anthems went very nicely and sounded especially well from the chancel. The moonlight came streaming in broadly through the chancel windows. When the choir had gone and the lights were out and the church quiet again, as the schoolmaster and his friend stood with me at the Church door in the moonlight we were remarking the curious fact that this year Good Friday like the Passover has fallen upon the 15th day of the month and the full moon. As I walked down the Churchyard alone the decked graves had a strange effect in the moonlight and looked as if the people had laid down to sleep for the night out of doors, ready dressed to rise early on Easter morning. I lingered in the verandah before going to bed. The air was as soft and warm as a summer night, and the broad moonlight made the quiet village almost as light as day. Everyone seemed to have gone to rest and there was not a sound except the clink and trickle of the brook.

Revd Francis Kilvert, *Diary*, 16 April 1870

♣ He who is born on Eastern morn will never know want or care or harm.

Kelmscott

Easter Monday [1889]

The country is about six weeks backward; more backward by a good deal than it was last year, though that was late: neither the big trees (except the chestnuts) nor the apple trees show any sign of life yet. The garden is very pretty, though there are scarcely any flowers in blossom except the primroses; but there are such beautiful promises of buds and things just out of the ground that it makes amends for all. The buds of the wild tulip, which is one of the beautifullest flowers there is,

just at point to open. Jenny and I went up to Buscot wood this morning: it is such a change from our river plain that it is like going into another country; yet I don't much care about a wood unless it is a very big one; and Buscot is scarcely more than a coppice; but the blue distance between the trunks was very beautiful. As to the weather, bearing in mind that things are so much behindhand, it is not bad. To-day has been March all over; rain-showers, hail, wind, dead calm, thunder, finishing with a calm frosty evening sky. The birds are amusing, especially the starlings, whereof there are many: but some damned fool has been bullying our rooks so much that they have only got six nests, so that we haven't got the proper volume of sound from them.

One grief, the sort of thing that is always happening in the spring: there were some beautiful willows at Eaton Hastings which to my certain knowledge had not been polled during the whole 17 years that we have been here; and now the idiot Parson has polled them into wretched stumps. I should like to cut off the beggar's legs and have wooden ones made for him out of the willow timber, the value of which is about 7s. 6d.

William Morris, letter to Mrs Burne-Jones, *Letters*,
ed. P. Henderson, 1950

April 20 [1874]—Young elmleaves lash and lip the sprays. This has been a very beautiful day—fields about us deep green lighted underneath with white daisies, yellower fresh green of leaves above which bathes the skirts of the elms, and their tops are touched and worded with leaf too. Looked at the big limb of that elm that hangs over into the Park at the swinggate/ further out than where the leaves were open and saw beautiful inscape, home-coiling wiry bushes of spray, touched with bud to point them. Blue shadows fell all up the meadow at sunset and then standing at the far Park corner my eye was struck by such a sense of green in the tufts and pashes of grass, with purple shadow thrown back on the dry black mould behind them, as I do not remember ever to have been exceeded in looking at green grass. I marked this down on a slip of paper at the time, because the eye for colour, rather the zest in the mind, seems to weaken with years, but now the paper is mislaid

April 25, Saturday, eve of the Feast of St. Joseph's Patronage Br.

Alexander Byrne died of rapid consumption. He was a novice but had been one of my pupils

The beginning of May very cold and so on to the 14th, I think—a mockery of bright sunshine day after day, no rain (Except that on one day there was hail and then a little rain), wind always holding from the north, dim blue skies, faint clouds, ashy frosts in the morning: saw young ivyleaves along the sunkfence bitten and blackened. There was something of a break, with rain, but still now it is cold (May 21)

May 7—To Kew Gardens with Br. Campbell the Highlander and Br. Younan a young Syrian from Calcutta. Did not see much but the mandarin duck. The Old Palace though is a pretty picture—ruddled red brick over a close-shaven green-white lawn; chestnuts in bloom and a beech in a fairy spray of green

I see how chestnuts in bloom look like big seeded strawberries

May 17—Bright. Took Br. Tournade to Combe Wood to see and gather bluebells, which we did, but fell in bluehanded with a gamekeeper, which is a humbling thing to do. Then we heard a nightingale utter a few strains—strings of very liquid gurgles.

Gerard Manley Hopkins, Journal

[*In Tuscany*]

In the pause towards the end of April, when the flowers seem to hesitate, the leaves make up their minds to come out. For some time, at the very ends of the bare boughs of fig trees, spurts of pure green have been burning like little cloven tongues of green fire vivid on the tips of the candelabrum. Now these spurts of green spread out, and begin to take the shape of hands, feeling for the air of summer. And tiny green figs are below them, like glands on the throat of a goat.

For some time, the long stiff whips of the vine have had knobby pink buds, like flower buds. Now these pink buds begin to unfold into greenish, half-shut fans of leaves with red in the veins, and tiny spikes of flower, like seed-pearls. Then, in all its down and pinky dawn, the vine-rosette has a frail, delicious scent of a new year.

Now the aspens on the hill are all remarkable with the translucent membranes of blood-veined leaves. They are gold-brown, but not like autumn, rather like the thin wings of bats when like birds—call them birds—they wheel in clouds against the setting sun, and the sun glows through the stretched membrane of their wings, as through thin, brown-red stained glass. This is the red sap of summer, not the red dust of autumn. And in the distance the aspens have the tender panting glow of living membrane just come awake. This is the beauty of the frailty of spring.

The cherry tree is something the same, but more sturdy. Now, in the last week of April, the cherry blossom is still white, but waning and passing away: it is late this year; and the leaves are clustering thick and softly copper in their dark blood-filled glow. It is queer about fruit trees in this district. The pear and the peach were out together. But now the pear tree is a lovely thick softness of new and glossy green, vivid with a tender fullness of apple-green leaves, gleaming among all the other green of the landscape, the half-high wheat, emerald, and the grey olive, half-invisible, the browning green of the dark cypress, the black of the evergreen oak, the rolling, heavy green puffs of the stone-pines, the flimsy green of small peach and almond trees, the sturdy young green of horse-chestnut. So many greens, all in flakes and shelves and tilted tables and round shoulders and plumes and shaggles and uprisen bushes, of greens and greens, sometimes blindingly brilliant at evening, when the landscape looks as if it were on fire from inside, with greenness and with gold.

The pear is perhaps the greenest thing in the landscape. The wheat may shine lit-up yellow, or glow bluish, but the pear tree is green in itself. The cherry has white, half-absorbed flowers, so has the apple. But the plum is rough with her new foliage, and inconspicuous, inconspicuous as the almond, the peach, the apricot, which one can no longer find in the landscape, though twenty days ago they were the distinguished pink individuals of the whole countryside. Now they are gone. It is the time of green, pre-eminent green, in ruffles and flakes and slabs.

In the wood, the scrub-oak is only just coming uncrumpled, and the pines keep their hold on winter. They are wintry things, stone-pines. At Christmas, their heavy green clouds are richly beautiful. When the cypresses raise their tall and naked bodies of dark green, and the osiers are vivid red-orange, on the still blue air, and the land is lavender; then, in mid-winter, the landscape is most beautiful in colour, surging with colour.

But now, when the nightingale is still drawing out his long, wistful, yearning, teasing plaint-note, and following it up with a rich and joyful burble, the pines and the cypresses seem hard and rusty, and the wood has lost its subtlety and its mysteriousness. It still seems wintry in spite of the yellowing young oaks, and the heath in flower. But hard, dull pines above, and hard, dull, tall heath below, all stiff and resistant, this is out of the mood of spring.

In spite of the fact that the stone-white heath is in full flower, and very lovely when you look at it, it does not, casually, give the impression of blossom. More the impression of having its tips and crests all dipped in hoarfrost; or in a whitish dust. It has a peculiar ghostly colourlessness amid the darkish colourlessness of the wood altogether, which completely takes away the sense of spring.

Yet the tall white heath is very lovely, in its invisibility. It grows sometimes as tall as a man, lifting up its spires and its shadowy-white fingers with a ghostly fullness, amid the dark, rusty green of its lower bushiness; and it gives off a sweet honeyed scent in the sun, and a cloud of fine white stone-dust, if you touch it. Looked at closely, its little bells are most beautiful, delicate and white, with the brown-purple inner eye and the dainty pin-head of the pistil. And out in the sun at the edge of the wood, where the heath grows tall and thrusts up its spires of dim white next a brilliant, yellow-flowering vetch-bush, under a blue sky, the effect has a real magic.

And yet, in spite of all, the dim whiteness of all the flowering heath-fingers only adds to the hoariness and out-of-date quality of the pine-woods, now in the pause between spring and summer. It is the ghost of the interval.

D. H. Lawrence, 'Flowery Tuscany', 1927, in *Selected Essays*

May

May comes up with tit-show
May comes up with a sneeze
May slips by with a whiff and a sigh
Blossom on the breeze

May comes up with windows
May lolls bare at ease
May burns brown as the sun goes down
Curtains in the breeze

May comes up with bunting
May was born to please
May rides high with a billowing sky
Candles on the trees

May comes up with visions
May knows how to tease
May goes by in the blink of an eye
Flaunting dappled dreams

Peter Forbes, The Aerial Noctiluca, 1981

♣ A hot May makes a fat churchyard.

The Mill,
West Milton
19 May 1970

Dearest Mandle,

Weather's sort of patchy here, but the countryside is incomparably beautiful. The wild flowers are surging along the hedge banks; ragged robin, lords and ladies, bluebells, hankbits—a blaze of colour. In our marshy meadow we've got a huge colony of marsh marigolds, which almost burn with yellowness. The dippers are nesting under our bridge! Haven't found the nest, but when Fabe was here two days ago I was taunted into going into the swimming pool (my limbs went blue with cold and I felt as if I'd been pumped full of anaesthetic but I did swim—Fabe chickened out, standing whimpering and whining on the side). We also threw Galadriel in—she hated it—and I went on crutches along the yew walk, and saw the dipper flip out from under the bridge. Then its mate came whizzing along with a beak full of food. I scrambled down into the stream and waded about on crutches, but couldn't find the nest. But rather super, isn't it, having dippers nesting in one's garden?

Kenneth Allsop, Letters to his Daughter, 1974

[*Mayday Celebrations*]

But their chiefest jewel they bring from thence is their maypole, which they bring home with great veneration, as thus: They have twenty or forty yoke of oxen, every ox having a sweet nosegay of flowers tied on the tip of his horns, and these oxen draw home this maypole (this stinking idol rather), which is covered all over with flowers and herbs, bound about with strings, from the top to the bottom, and sometimes painted with variable colours, with two or three hundred men, women and children following it, with great devotion. And thus being reared up, with handkerchiefs and flags streaming at the top, they strew the ground about, bind green boughs about it, set up summer halls, bowers and arbours hard by it. And then they fall to banquet and feast, to leap and dance about it, as the heathen people did, at the dedication of their idols, whereof this is a perfect pattern, or rather the thing itself.

Philip Stubbes, 16th-century Puritan

♣ A swarm of bees in May is worth a load of hay.

Selborne, May 12, 1770.

Last month we had such a series of cold turbulent weather, such a constant succession of frost, and snow, and hail, and tempest, that the regular migration or appearance of the summer birds was much interrupted. Some did not show themselves (at least were not heard) till weeks after their usual time; as the black-cap and white-throat; and some have not been heard yet, as the grasshopper-lark and largest willow-wren. As to the fly-catcher, I have not seen it; it is indeed one of the latest, but should appear about this time: and yet, amidst all this meteorous strife and war of the elements, two swallows discovered themselves as long ago as the eleventh of April, in frost and snow; but they withdrew quickly, and were not visible again for many days. House-martins, which are always more backward than swallows, were not observed till May came in.

Gilbert White, *The Natural History of Selborne*, 1789

♣ Shear your sheep in May, and shear them all away.

The swallows come, it is said, with great secrecy, and go with great secrecy! So does the heavy woodcock;—and yet no one ever doubted of the migration of that plethoric bird, whose unusual flight is not many hundred yards. A few are sometimes seen after the rest have departed, on the breaking out of a few fine days; and a few which, in spring appear first, as suddenly disappear on the return of cold. Can this be any wonder in birds of such velocity? Some however have been found in a dormant state here. This is a fact;—but a fact *only* of a few, and of rare occurrence; and proves no more than that, when accident prevents their departure, nature has given them the power of so existing. But of all the absurd hypotheses broached on this head, that of their remaining at the bottom of pools and marshes under water, during winter, is the most preposterous. Dissection has proved that they have no organic provision for such a state, and could not live half an hour in submersion; so that we are obliged to sacrifice our love of the marvellous and mysterious, and to let the poor birds go, as Nature has given them power, to the southern lands of summer.

William Howitt, *Book of the Seasons*, 1833

Swifts

Fifteenth of May. Cherry blossom. The swifts
Materialise at the tip of a long scream
Of needle. 'Look! They're back! Look!' And they're gone
On a steep

Controlled scream of skid
Round the house-end and away under the cherries. Gone.
Suddenly flickering in sky summit, three or four together,
Gnat-whisp frail, and hover-searching, and listening

For air-chills—are they too early? With a bowing
Power-thrust to left, then to right, then a flicker they
Tilt into a slide, a tremble for balance,
Then a lashing down disappearance

Behind elms.
               They've made it again,
Which means the globe's still working, the Creation's
Still waking refreshed, our summer's
Still all to come—
               And here they are, here they are again
Erupting across yard stones
Shrapnel-scatter terror. Frog-gapers,
Speedway goggles, international mobsters—

A bolas of three or four wire screams
Jockeying across each other
On their switchback wheel of death.
They swat past, hard-fletched,

Veer on the hard air, toss up over the roof,
And are gone again. Their mole-dark labouring,
Their lunatic limber scramming frenzy
And their whirling blades

Sparkle out into blue—
               Not ours any more.
Rats ransacked their nests so now they shun us.
Round luckier houses now
They crowd their evening dirt-track meetings,

Racing their discords, screaming as if speed-burned,
Head-height, clipping the doorway
With their leaden velocity and their butterfly lightness,
Their too much power, their arrow-thwack into the eaves.

Every year a first-fling, nearly-flying
Misfit flopped in our yard,
Groggily somersaulting to get airborne.
He bat-crawled on his tiny useless feet, tangling his flails

Like a broken toy, and shrieking thinly
Till I tossed him up—then suddenly he flowed away under
His bowed shoulders of enormous swimming power,
Slid away along levels wobbling

On the fine wire they have reduced life to,
And crashed among the raspberries.
Then followed fiery hospital hours
In a kitchen. The moustached goblin savage

Nested in a scarf. The bright blank
Blind, like an angel, to my meat-crumbs and flies.
Then eyelids resting. Wasted clingers curled.
The inevitable balsa death.

                            Finally burial
For the husk
Of my little Apollo—

The charred scream
Folded in its huge power.

Ted Hughes, *Season Songs*, 1976

Set off with Spencer and Leonard Cowper at 2 o'clock for Mouse
Castle. By the fields to Hay, then to Llydiart-y-Wain. It is years since I
have seen this house and I had quite forgotten how prettily it is
situated. At least it looked very pretty today bosomed among its white
blossoming fruit trees, the grey fruitful homestead with its two large
gleaming ponds. Thence up a steep meadow to the left and by some
quarries, over a stile in a wire fence and up a lovely winding path
through the woods spangled with primroses and starred with wood
anemones among trees and bushes thickening green. It was very hot in
the shelter of the woods as we climbed up. The winding path led us

round to the back of the hill till at last we emerged into a bold green brow in the middle of which stood a square steep rampart of grey crumbling sandstone rock with a flat top covered with grass bushes and trees, a sort of small wood. This rampart seemed about 15 feet high. The top of the hill round the base of the rampart undulated in uneven swells and knolls with little hillocks covered with short downy grass. One of the knolls overlooking the wooded side of the hill towards Hay was occupied by a wild group. A stout elderly man in a velveteen jacket with a walking stick sat or lay upon the dry turf. Beside him sat one or two young girls, while two or three more girls and boys climbed up and down an accessible point in the rampart like young wild goats, swarmed up into the hazel trees on the top of the rock and sat in the forks and swung. I could not make the party out at all. They were not poor and they certainly were not rich. They did not look like farmers, cottagers or artizans. They were perfectly nondescript, seemed to have come from nowhere and to be going nowhere, but just to have fallen from the sky upon Mouse Castle, and to be just amusing themselves. The girls about 12 or 14 years old climbed up the steep rocks before and just above us quite regardless of the shortness of their petticoats and the elevating and inflating powers of the wind. We climbed up too and found no castle or ruin of one. Nothing but hazels and bushes. A boy was seated in the fork of one hazel and a girl swinging in the wind in another. We soon came down again covered with dust and went to repose upon an inviting knoll green sunny and dry, from which two girls jumped up and ran away with needless haste. The man lay down in the grass on his face and apparently went to sleep. The girls called him 'Father'. They were full of fun and larks as wild as hawks, and presently began a great romp on the grass which ended in their rolling and tumbling head over heels and throwing water over each other and pouring some cautiously on their father's head. Then they scattered primroses over him. Next the four girls danced away down the path to a spring in the wood with a pitcher to draw more water, leaving a little girl and little boy with their father. We heard the girls shrieking with laughter and screaming with fun down below at the spring in the wood as they romped and, no doubt, threw water over each other and pushed each other into the spring. Presently they re-appeared on the top with the pitcher, laughing and struggling, and again the romp began. They ran after each other flinging water in showers, throwing each other down and rolling over on the grass. Seeing us amused and laughing they became still more wild and excited. They were fine good looking spirited girls all of them. But there were one or two quite pretty and one in a red frock was the wildest and most reckless of the troop. In the romp her dress was torn open all down her back, but whilst one of her sisters was trying to fasten it for her she burst away and tore it all open again showing vast spaces of white, skin as well as linen. Meanwhile the water that had been ostensibly fetched up from the spring to drink had all been thrown wantonly away, some carefully poured over their father, the rest wildly dashed at each other, up the clothes, over the head down the neck and back, anywhere except down their own throats. Someone pretended to be thirsty and to lament that all the water was gone so the whole bevy trooped merrily off down to the spring again.

Revd Francis Kilvert, *Diary*, 19 April 1870

SUMMER

THIS is the time of year when the Protestant work-ethic is at its weakest, most vulnerable. Few of us can honestly deny that we associate the season with the pleasures of the outdoors, and especially the delights of doing nothing in particular. An epidemic of sun-worship breaks out; dress diminishes; we go unprotected. And, of course, its stay is all too short.

Seriousness, serious thought, serious affairs, suffer a welcome eclipse, and even the English can be seen smiling and talking to strangers. We are responding, of course, to the prodigality of nature; and bringing out our euphemisms, so that when it rains, we talk of 'showers'.

Television falls into desuetude, and gardens come into their own, loud with the racket of electrified machinery, and the snore of those who turn pink in their deckchairs.

Our limbs no longer need to fidget in order to keep warm, but stretch themselves expansively like summer landscapes; after the almost frenetic energy of spring, we find ourselves a slower pulse, a deeper steadier rhythm. This amplitude perhaps is where we really live, where we have our being; at such a time the other seasons seem to be merely preludes, postludes, or mistakes.

MAY: May somehow goes by before I have time to notice what Nature's doing on the recreation ground, let alone get tickets to fail to notice it elsewhere. *June*'s the month, of course. Midsummer; full leaf; the fresh prime of the year. To hell with the tawdry pleasures of foreign cities—in June I will take a knapsack and a stout stick and stride through the heartlands of England. Through Warwickshire, Worcestershire, Gloucestershire, Oxfordshire; through old towns full of bells and strong ale; through ancient green forests where temporarily dispossessed dukes wander with their courts, hunting the deer and communing in blank verse as fresh as spring-water.

JUNE: Take up my stout umbrella and stride through the heartlands of the recreation ground, now gaily bedecked with the Lesser and Greater Paper Bag, the Common Orangeskin, and the shyly peeping Lolly Stick.   Michael Frayn, *At Bay in Gear Street*, 1967

What I like best is to lie whole mornings on a sunny bank on Salisbury Plain.   William Hazlitt, *On a Sun-Dial*, 1839

I had been staying with a friend of mine, an artist and delightfully lazy fellow, at his cottage among the Yorkshire fells, some ten miles from a railway-station; and as we had been fortunate enough to encounter a sudden spell of really warm weather, day after day we had set off in the morning, taken the nearest moorland track, climbed leisurely until we had reached somewhere about two thousand feet above sea-level, and had then spent long golden afternoons lying flat on our backs—doing nothing. There is no better lounging place than a moor. It is a kind of clean bare antechamber to heaven. Beneath its apparent monotony that offers no immediate excitements, no absorbing drama of sound and colour, there is a subtle variety in its slowly changing patterns of cloud and shadow and tinted horizons, sufficient to keep up a flicker of interest in the mind all day. With its velvety patches, no bigger than a drawing-room carpet, of fine moorland grass, its surfaces invite repose. Its remoteness, its permanence, its old and sprawling indifference to man and his concerns, rest and cleanse the mind. All the noises of the world are drowned in the one monotonous cry of the curlew.

J. B. Priestley, 'On Doing Nothing', *Open House*, 1934

> Nor shall the Muse disdain
> To let the little noisy summer-race
> Live in her lay, and flutter through her song:
> Not mean, though simple; to the sun ally'd,
> From him they draw their animating fire.
>
> Wak'd by his warmer ray, the reptile young
> Come wing'd abroad; by the light air upborne,
> Lighter, and full of soul. From every chink,
> And secret corner, where they slept away
> The wintry storms; or rising from their tombs,
> To higher life; by myriads, forth at once,
> Swarming they pour; all of the vary'd hues
> Their beauty-beaming parent can disclose,
> Ten thousand forms, ten thousand different tribes,
> People the blaze. To sunny waters some
> By fatal instinct fly; where on the pool
> They, sportive, wheel: or, sailing down the stream,
> Are snatch'd immediate by the quick-ey'd trout,
> Or darting salmon. Through the green-wood glade
> Some love to stray; there lodg'd, amus'd, and fed,
> In the fresh leaf. Luxurious, others make
> The meads of their choice, and visit every flower,
> And every latent herb: for the sweet task,
> To propagate their kinds, and where to wrap,
> In what soft beds, their young yet undisclos'd,
> Employs their tender care. Some to the house,
> The fold, and dairy, hungry, bend their flight;
> Sip round the pail, or taste the curdling cheese;
> Oft, inadvertent, from the milky stream
> They meet their fate; or, weltering in the bowl,
> With powerless wings around them wrapt, expire.

James Thomson, from *The Seasons*, 1726–30

May 29, 1882

I hope you are making use of this fine weather to get out on the Heath
and enjoy the glorious colours of earth and sky. Yesterday I had a long
walk with a friend out to Richmond Park, and saw some of the most

beautiful country scenery one could wish to revel amongst. In the midst of the splendid woods and fields which border the Thames in that part, one would think any large town was at least a hundred miles away.

It is Bank Holiday today, and the streets are overcrowded with swarms of people. Never is so clearly to be seen the vulgarity of the people as at these holiday times. Their notion of a holiday is to rush in crowds to some sweltering place, such as the Crystal Palace, and there sit and drink and quarrel themselves into stupidity. Miserable children are lugged about, yelling at the top of their voices, and are beaten because they yell. Troops of hideous creatures drive wildly about the town in gigs, donkey-carts, cabbage-carts, dirt-carts, and think it enjoyment. The pleasure of peace and quietness, of rest for body and mind, is not understood. Thousands are tempted by cheap trips to go off for the day to the seaside, and succeed in wearying themselves to death, for the sake of eating a greasy meal in a Margate Coffee-shop, and getting five minutes' glimpse of the sea through eyes blinded with dirt and perspiration. Places like Hampstead Heath and the various parks and commons are packed with screeching drunkards, one general mass of dust and heat and rage and exhaustion. Yet this is the best kind of holiday the people are capable of.

It is utterly absurd, this idea of setting aside single days for great public holidays. It will never do anything but harm. What we want is a general shortening of working hours all the year round, so that, for instance, all labour would be over at 4 o'clock in the afternoon. Then the idea of hours of leisure would become familiar to the people and they would learn to make some sensible use of them. Of course this is impossible so long as we work for working's sake. All the world's work—all that is really necessary for the health and comfort and even luxury of mankind—could be performed in three or four hours each day. There is so much labour just because there is so much money-grubbing. Every man has to fight for a living with his neighbour, and the grocer who keeps his shop open till half an hour after midnight has an advantage over him who closes at twelve. Work in itself is *not an end*; *only a means*; but we nowadays make it an end, and three-fourths of the world cannot understand anything else.

George Gissing, *Letters of George Gissing*, 1927

These June evenings, when for once in a way we are allowed a deep warm sloping sunlight, how rare and how precious they are. They ought to be accompanied by fireflies, wild gold flakes in the air, but in this island we have to make do with tethered flowers instead. Amongst these, the huge lax bushes of the old roses must take an honoured place.

The old roses have recently wriggled their way back into favour, and small wonder. They give so little trouble for so great a reward. By the old roses I mean the Cabbage, the Moss, the Centifolias, the Gallicas, the Musks and the Damasks whose very names suggest a honeyed southern dusk.   *V. Sackville-West's Garden Book*, 1974

♣ A swarm of bees in June is worth a silver spoon.

After I did mind the baby and sleeps was come upon it, then I did walk into the garden. I went there to find out how much things had grown since last time I was there. First I pulled up a bean plant. It looked a little more big—the two peek-a-boo leaves did. After I looked close looks at it, I did plant it again. Then I pulled up a radish. It was doing nicely and I ate it. I forgot to give it close looks before I put it in my mouth to see how much it did grow since that last time. After I swallowed it, I pulled up another radish to find out. It was doing well. I put it back in the garden again and I went to the house and got it a drink of buttermilk. I carried it out to it in the papa's shaving-mug. There was more drink than one radish needs, so I did give four onions and two more radishes sips of buttermilk. And I did give to the papa's shaving-mug some washes in the brook, and I put it back in its place on the shelf again.   Opal Whiteley, *Diary*, 1920

Summer

Winter is cold-hearted,
Spring is yea and nay,
Autumn is a weathercock
Blown every way.
Summer days for me
When every leaf is on its tree;

When Robin's not a beggar,
  And Jenny Wren's a bride,
And larks hang singing, singing, singing
    Over the wheat-fields wide,
    And anchored lilies ride,
    And the pendulum spider
    Swings from side to side;

And blue-black beetles transact business,
    And gnats fly in a host,
And furry caterpillars hasten
    That no time be lost,
    And moths grow fat and thrive,
    And ladybirds arrive.

  Before green apples blush,
  Before green nuts embrown,
  Why one day in the country
  Is worth a month in town;
  Is worth a day and a year
Of the dusty, musty, lag-last fashion
  That days drone elsewhere.

Robert Herrick (1591–1674)

♣ Calm weather in June sets corn in tune.

The children were at the theatre, acting to Three Cows as much as they could remember of *Midsummer Night's Dream*. Their father had made them a small play out of the big Shakespeare one, and they had rehearsed it with him and with their mother till they could say it by heart. They began where Nick Bottom the weaver comes out of the bushes with a donkey's head on his shoulder, and finds Titania Queen of the Fairies asleep. Then they skipped to the part where Bottom asks three little fairies to scratch his head and bring him honey, and they ended where he falls asleep in Titania's arms. Dan was Puck and Nick Bottom, as well as all three fairies. He wore a pointy-eared cloth cap for Puck, and a paper donkey's head out of a Christmas cracker—but it tore if you were not careful—for Bottom. Una was Titania, with a wreath of columbines and a foxglove wand.

The theatre lay in a meadow called the Long Slip. A little mill-stream, carrying water to a mill two or three fields away, bent round one corner of it, and in the middle of the bend lay a large old fairy-ring of darkened grass, which was the stage. The mill-stream banks, overgrown with willow, hazel, and guelder-rose, made convenient places to wait in till your turn came; and a grown-up who had seen it said that Shakespeare himself could not have imagined a more suitable setting for his play. They were not, of course, allowed to act on Midsummer Night itself, but they went down after tea on Midsummer Eve, when the shadows were growing, and they took their supper—hard-boiled eggs, Bath Oliver biscuits, and salt in an envelope—with them. Three Cows had been milked and were grazing steadily with a tearing noise that one could hear all down the meadow; and the noise of the mill at work sounded like bare feet running on hard ground. A cuckoo sat on a gate-post singing his broken June tune, 'cuckoo-cuk,' while a busy kingfisher crossed from the mill-stream to the brook which ran on the other side of the meadow. Everything else was a sort of thick, sleepy stillness smelling of meadow-sweet and dry grass.

Rudyard Kipling, *Puck of Pook's Hill*, 1906

So, some tempestuous morn in early June,
   When the year's primal burst of bloom is o'er,
      Before the roses and the longest day—
   When garden-walks, and all the grassy floor,
      With blossoms, red and white, of fallen May,
         And chestnut-flowers are strewn—
   So have I heard the cuckoo's parting cry,
      From the wet field, through the vext garden-trees,
      Come with the volleying rain and tossing breeze:
   The bloom is gone, and with the bloom go I.

Too quick despairer, wherefore wilt thou go?
    Soon will the high Midsummer pomps come on,
        Soon will the musk carnations break and swell,
    Soon shall we have gold-dusted snapdragon,
        Sweet-William with its homely cottage-smell,
            And stocks in fragrant blow;
    Roses that down the alleys shine afar,
        And open, jasmine-muffled lattices,
        And groups under the dreaming garden-trees,
    And the full moon, and the white evening-star.

Matthew Arnold, from 'Thyrsis', 1867

They drove out immediately after breakfast, on one of those high mornings of the bared bosom of June when distances are given to our eyes, and a soft air fondles leaf and grassblade, and beauty and peace are overhead, reflected, if we will. Rain had fallen in the night. Here and there hung a milkwhite cloud with folded sail. The south-west left it in its bay of blue, and breathed below. At moments the fresh scent of herb and mould swung richly in warmth. The young beech-leaves glittered, pools of rain-water made the roadways laugh, the grass-banks under hedges rolled their interwoven weeds in cascades of many-shaded green to right and left of the pair of dappled ponies, and a squirrel crossed ahead, a lark went up a little way to ease his heart, closing his wings when the burst was over. Startled blackbirds, darting with a clamour like a broken cockcrow, looped the wayside woods from hazel to oak-scrub; short flights, quick spirits everywhere, steady sunshine above.

Diana held the reins. The whip was an ornament, as the plume of feathers to the general officer. Lady Dunstane's ponies were a present from Redworth, who always chose the pick of the land for his gifts. They joyed in their trot, and were the very love-birds of the breed for their pleasure of going together, so like that Diana called them the Dromios. Through an old gravel-cutting a gateway led to the turf of the down, springy turf bordered on a long line, clear as a racecourse, by golden gorse covers, and leftward over the gorse the dark ridge of the fir and heath country ran companionably to the south-west, the valley between, with undulations of wood and meadow sunned or shaded, clumps, mounds, promontories, away to broad spaces of tillage banked by wooded hills, and dimmer beyond and farther, the faintest shadowiness of heights, as a veil to the illimitable. Yews, junipers, radiant beeches, and gleams of the service-tree or the white-beam spotted the semicircle of swelling green Down black and silver. The sun in the valley sharpened his beams on squares of buttercups, and made a pond a diamond.

George Meredith, *Diana of the Crossways*, 1885

Summer was also the time of these: of sudden plenty, of slow hours and actions, of diamond haze and dust on the eyes, of the valley in post-vernal slumber; of burying birds out of seething corruption; of Mother sleeping heavily at noon; of jazzing wasps and dragonflies, haystooks and thistle-seeds, snows of white butterflies, skylark's eggs, bee-orchids, and frantic ants; of wolf-cub parades, and boy scouts' bugles; of sweat running down the legs; of boiling potatoes on bramble fires, of flames glass-blue in the sun; of lying naked in the hill-cold stream; begging pennies for bottles of pop; of girl's bare arms and unripe cherries, green apples and liquid walnuts; of fights and falls and new-scabbed knees, sobbing pursuits and flights; of picnics high up in the crumbling quarries, of butter running like oil, of sunstroke, fever, and cucumber peel stuck cool to one's burning brow. All this, and the feeling that it would never end, that such days had come for ever, with the pump drying up and the water-butt crawling, and the chalk ground hard as the moon. All sights twice-brilliant and smells twice-sharp, all game-days twice as long. Double charged as we were, like meadow ants, with the frenzy of the sun, we used up the light to its last violet drop, and even then couldn't go to bed.

Laurie Lee, *Cider with Rosie*, 1959

Summer Moods

I love at eventide to walk alone
Down narrow lanes oerhung with dewy thorn
Where from the long grass underneath the snail
Jet black creeps out and sprouts his timid horn
I love to muse oer meadows newly mown
Where withering grass perfumes the sultry air
Where bees search round with sad and weary drone
In vain for flowers that bloomed but newly there
While in the juicey corn the hidden quail
Cries 'wet my foot' and hid as thoughts unborn
The fairy like and seldom-seen land rail
Utters 'craik craik' like voices underground
Right glad to meet the evenings dewy veil
And see the light fade into glooms around

John Clare (1793–1864)

Cut Grass

Cut grass lies frail:
Brief is the breath
Mown stalks exhale.
Long, long the death

It dies in the white hours
Of young-leafed June
With chestnut flowers,
With hedges snowlike strewn,

White lilac bowed,
Lost lanes of Queen Anne's lace,
And that high-builded cloud
Moving at summer's pace.

Philip Larkin, *High Windows*, 1974

67

Evening primrose, nicotina (tobacco flower) and night-scented stock all appear half-closed during the day. They open towards evening and often remain open until about 10 a.m., so that children can see them both open and closed during school hours. All these are hardy and self-seeding and can fill up a patch in the school garden. In the country, various hawkweeds and sow-thistles close at some time during the day, especially the elegant 'John-go-to-bed-at-noon'.

Many summer flowers are sensitive to cold and wet, and close under these conditions; among them are: (garden), pink oxalis, tulip, anemone, sunflower, marguerite, rock-rose, gentian; (wild), pink centaury, scarlet pimpernel, daisy, speedwell, dandelion. Children can make coloured sketches of these flowers when open and closed, with date, time of day and weather condition at the time.

E. M. Stephenson, *Nature Study and Rural Science*,
A Four Year Course for Juniors, 1966

BROOM

This dark green and gold plant was once the badge of a mighty dynasty of English kings, who also adopted its medieval title— *Planta genista*—as their family name. Carved sprigs of broom decorate the effigy of the tragic King Richard II—Richard Plantagenet—which lies beside that of his queen in Westminster Abbey.

In contrast, the shrub's more usual name is applied to one of the humblest of domestic tools. Bound together in bunches, the tough, springy twigs were for centuries used to sweep floors.

Equally at home, therefore, in cottage and castle, the 'bonnie yellow broom' makes an early summer blaze on sandy heathlands throughout Europe.

The flowers have been used for many purposes: as an emblem of love, for instance, and as the base of a traditional country wine. In Yorkshire, they were mashed with lard to make an ointment for cuts on fishermen's hands.

A recipe of perhaps more general usefulness is to gather the buds in spring and pack them into jars with vinegar or salt. Thus pickled, they can be served in salads as an alternative to capers.

Infused, dried broom flowers also make a refreshing tea. Henry VIII considered this an excellent 'remedy for surfeits'.

'Food From Your Garden', 1977

June 28, 1665.

After 7 aclock in the evening there was almost a continued thunder until 8, wherein the *Tonitru and Fulgur*, the noise and lightning were so terrible that they put the whole city into an amazement, and most unto their prayers. The clouds went low and the cracks seemed near over our heads during the most part of the thunder.

About 8 aclock an *Ignis Fulmineus, pila ignea fulminians, Telum igneum fulmineum* or fire ball hit against the little wooden pinnacle of the high Leucome window of my house toward the market place, brake the flewboards and carried peices thereof a stones cast of; whereupon many of the tiles fell into the street and the windows in adjoining houses were broken. At the same time either a part of that close bound fire or another of the same nature fell into the courtyard and whereof no notice was taken till we began to examine the house, and then we found a freestone on the outside of the wall of the entry leading to the kitchen, half a foot from the ground, fallen from the wall, an hole as big as a football bored through the wall which is above a foot thick, and a chest which stood against it on the inside split and carried above a foot from the wall. The wall also behind the leaden cistern at 5 yards distance from it broken on the inside and outside, the middle seeming entire. The lead on the edges of the cistern turned a little up, and a great washing bowl that stood by it to receive the rain turned upside down and split quite thorough. Some chimneys and tiles were struck down in other parts of the city. A fire ball also flew down the walk in the market place. And all this god be thanked without mischief unto any person. The greatest terror from the noise, answerable unto 2 or 3 canons. The smell it left was strong like that after the discharge of a canon. The balls that flew were not like fire in the flame, but the coal, and the people said twas like the sun. It was *discutiens, terebrans,* but not *urens.* It burnt nothing, nor anything it touched smelt of fire, nor melted any lead of window or cistern, as I found it to do in the great storm about 2 years ago at Melton hall 4 miles of, at that time when the hail broke 3 thousand pounds worth of glass in Norwich in half a quarter of an hour. About four days after, the like fulmineous fire killed a man in Erpingham church by Aylisham, upon whom it brake and beat down divers which were within the wind of it. One also went of in Sr John Hobarts gallerie at Blickling: he was so near that his arm and thigh were numbed above an hour after. 2 or 3 days after a woman and horse were killed near Bungay; her hat so shivered that no peice remained bigger then a groat, whereof I had some peices sent unto me. Granadas, crakers and squibbs do much resemble the discharge, and *Aurum Fulminans* the fury thereof. Of other thunderbolts or *Lapides Fulminei* I have litle opinion: some I have by me under that name, but they are *e genere fossilium*.

Sir Thomas Browne

Haymaking

After night's thunder far away had rolled
The fiery day had a kernel sweet of cold,
And in the perfect blue the clouds uncurled,
Like the first gods before they made the world
And misery, swimming the stormless sea
In beauty and in divine gaiety.
The smooth white empty road was lightly strewn
With leaves—the holly's Autumn falls in June—
And fir cones standing stiff up in the heat.
The mill-foot water tumbled white and lit
With tossing crystals, happier than any crowd
Of children pouring out of school aloud.
And in the little thickets where a sleeper
For ever might lie lost, the nettle-creeper
And garden warbler sang unceasingly;
While over them shrill shrieked in his fierce glee
The swift with wings and tail as sharp and narrow
As if the bow had flown off with the arrow.

Only the scent of woodbine and hay new-mown
Travelled the road. In the field sloping down,
Park-like, to where its willows showed the brook,
Haymakers rested. The tosser lay forsook
Out in the sun; and the long waggon stood
Without its team; it seemed it never would
Move from the shadow of that single yew.
The team, as still, until their task was due,
Beside the labourers enjoyed the shade
That three squat oaks mid-field together made
Upon a circle of grass and weed uncut,
And on the hollow, once a chalk-pit, but
Now brimmed with nut and elder-flower so clean.
The men leaned on their rakes, about to begin,
But still. And all were silent. All was old,
This morning time, with a great age untold,
Older than Clare and Cowper, Morland and Crome,
Than, at the field's far edge, the farmer's home,
A white house crouched at the foot of a great tree.
Under the heavens that know not what years be
The men, the beasts, the trees, the implements
Uttered even what they will in times far hence—
All of us gone out of the reach of change—
Immortal in a picture of an old grange.

Edward Thomas, 1915

When the hay was all cleared it was soon time to think about harvest. But in between came mangle and cabbage hoeing. This also was done piece work £1.0.0 per acre to flat hoe twice over, then flat hoe again and set out. We used to grow a good quantity of mangle and cabbage for the cow's winter feed. About twenty acres of mangle and twelve to fifteen acres of cabbage so this kept the men busy until it was time to think of harvest.

In them days we had to cut a lot of our corn by hand. Self-binders were just coming in, but we had three reaping machines and we had to get 'swoppers' from Kent. The reapers were a machine drawn by three horses—two in the shafts and a trace-horse in front with a boy riding to guide it round the corners. It had a table to hold the corn as it was cut and five rakes went round and round to lay corn on to the table and you could adjust it to make one of the rakes slide it off the table in a wad. We used to throw out at every third rake which was about the size of a binder sheaf. If the straw was a good length you could put two wads in one sheaf, but it made hard work for the boys loading—also for the feeder when threshing. These machines would cut about six acres a day. The first binder ever I saw was a big wooden box arrangement, made by Hornsby's, and took four horses to pull it in double tandem fashion and a boy rode on one of the front two to get them round the corners. As with reaping, it was not a very big success at first—too big and cumbersome. It would tie one sheaf and miss two. But they soon made an improvement and turned out a nice little all steel framed binder with a much more reliable knitter and a 5′ 6″ cut.

These swoppers from Kent used to come every year regular. There was old George Reed who used to bring the whole family—mother, three sons and a daughter and make it their holiday . . .

Bob Copper, A Song for Every Season, 1971

WEDNESDAY 15TH JUNE

It is dry, but still not warm enough to promise any hay harvesting in the next few days. But we want to be ready when the time comes, so David serviced the mower. John has already bought the baler cord. The baler itself was checked over this afternoon, parts replaced where necessary and greased up. Just the hay turner and the elevator to see to and we shall be ready.

The milk yield is around 160 and rising, and with the machine working well now, and David back, life is easier for everyone. From tomorrow we shall be able to send away both Marigold and Lucille's milk and that will boost the yield. The last of the dry cows, due to calve in August has gone up to Parsonage, so we should hover around the 160–170 gallon mark for most of the summer.

THURSDAY 16TH

Another day waiting for the warm weather. Graham went weed-cutting down on the Marsh around the hedges.

Michael Morpurgo, All Around the Year, 1979

♣ Thistles cut in May
Come again next day.
Thistles cut in June
Come up again soon.
Cut them in July,
They'll be sure to die.

It was a typical summer evening in June, the atmosphere being in such delicate equilibrium and so transmissive that inanimate objects seemed endowed with two or three senses, if not five. There was no distinction between the near and the far, and an auditor felt close to everything within the horizon. The soundlessness impressed her as a positive entity rather than as the mere negation of noise. It was broken by the strumming of strings.

Tess had heard those notes in the attic above her head. Dim, flattened, constrained by their confinement, they had never appealed to her as now, when they wandered in the still air with a stark quality like that of nudity. To speak absolutely, both instrument and execution were poor; but the relative is all, and as she listened Tess, like a fascinated bird, could not leave the spot. Far from leaving she drew up towards the performer, keeping behind the hedge that he might not guess her presence.

The outskirt of the garden in which Tess found herself had been left uncultivated for some years, and was now damp and rank with juicy grass which sent up mists of pollen at a touch; and with tall blooming weeds emitting offensive smells—weeds whose red and yellow and purple hues formed a polychrome as dazzling as that of cultivated flowers. She went stealthily as a cat through this profusion of growth, gathering cuckoo-spittle on her skirts, cracking snails that were underfoot, staining her hands with thistle-milk and slug-slime, and rubbing off upon her naked arms sticky blights which, though snow-white on the apple-tree trunks, made blood-red stains on her skin; thus she drew quite near to Clare, still unobserved of him.

Tess was conscious of neither time nor space. The exaltation which she had described as being producible at will by gazing at a star, came now without any determination of hers; she undulated upon the thin notes of the second-hand harp, and their harmonies passed like breezes through her, bringing tears into her eyes. The floating pollen seemed to be his notes made visible, and the dampness of the garden the weeping of the garden's sensibility. Though near nightfall, the rank-smelling weed-flowers glowed as if they would not close for intentness, and the waves of colour mixed with the waves of sound.

The light which still shone was derived entirely from a large hole in the western bank of cloud; it was like a piece of day left behind by accident, dusk having closed in elsewhere. He concluded his plaintive melody, a very simple performance, demanding no great skill; and she waited, thinking another might be begun. But, tired of playing, he had desultorily come round the fence, and was rambling up behind her. Tess, her cheeks on fire, moved away furtively, as if hardly moving at all.

Thomas Hardy, Tess of the D'Urbervilles, 1891

Then began the hum of conning over lessons and getting them by heart, the whispered jest and stealthy game, and all the noise and drawl of school; and in the midst of the din sat the poor schoolmaster, the very image of meekness and simplicity, vainly attempting to fix his mind upon the duties of the day . . . his thoughts were rambling from his pupils—it was plain.

None knew this better than the idlest boys, who, growing bolder with impunity, waxed louder and more daring; playing odd-or-even under the master's eye, eating apples openly and without rebuke, pinching each other in sport or malice without the least reserve, and cutting their autographs in the very legs of his desk. The puzzled dunce, who stood beside it to say his lesson out of book, looked no longer at the ceiling for forgotten words, but drew closer to the master's elbow and boldly cast his eye upon the page; the wag of the little troop squinted and made grimaces (at the smallest boy, of course), holding no book before his face, and his approving audience knew no constraint in their delight. If the master did chance to rouse himself and seem alive to what was going on, the noise subsided for a moment and no eyes met his but wore a studious and a deeply humble look; but the instant he relapsed again, it broke out afresh, and ten times louder than before.

Oh! how some of those idle fellows longed to be outside, and how they looked at the open door and window, as if they half meditated rushing violently out, plunging into the woods, and being wild boys and savages from that time forth. What rebellious thoughts of the cool river, and some shady bathing-place beneath willow trees with branches dipping in the water, kept tempting and urging that sturdy boy, who, with his shirt-collar unbuttoned and flung back as far as it could go, sat fanning his flushed face with a spelling-book, wishing himself a whale, or a tittlebat, or a fly, or anything but a boy at school on that hot, broiling day! Heat! ask that other boy, whose seat being nearest to the door gave him opportunities of gliding out into the garden and driving his companions to madness by dipping his face into the bucket of the well and then rolling on the grass—ask him if there were ever such a day as that, when even the bees were diving deep down into the cups of flowers and stopping there, as if they had made up their minds to retire from business and be manufacturers of honey no more. The day was made for laziness, and lying on one's back in green places, and staring at the sky till its brightness forced one to shut one's eyes and go to sleep; and was this a time to be poring over musty books in a dark room, slighted by the very sun itself? Monstrous!

Charles Dickens, *The Old Curiosity Shop*, 1841

I have opened the window to warm my hands on the sill
Where the sunlight soaks in the stone: the afternoon
Is full of dreams, my love; the boys are all still
In a wishful dream of Lorna Doone.

The clink of the shunting engines is sharp and fine
Like savage music striking far off; and away
On the uplifted blue Palace, light pools stir and shine
Where the glass is domed by the blue, soft day.

D. H. Lawrence, from 'Dreams Old and Nascent', *Early Poems*, 1908

Not a drop of lamp oil,
Not a drop of pet-rol,
Not an inch of can-dle,
Oh-what-mis-er-y!

Hopping from one foot to the other and singing as loud as she can, Bel-Gazou is propagating the expression of the sad truth. It is a fact:

there's a dearth of lamp oil at Brive and at Varets, petrol has vanished, candles cost four francs twenty-five the pound, and are becoming scarce . . .

> Not a drop of lamp oil,
> Not a drop of pet-rol . . .

Bel-Gazou, bathed in sunlight, ironically proclaims the general bereavement of artificial lights. June is ending, and she is tanned like a Breton fisherman. My nose, caught with a sunburn, is peeling, while her nose is syncretized with her cheeks by colours borrowed from bronzes, ceramics, glossy fruit, and I am envious. Her bare gypsy feet thud upon the flagstones and on the old parquet. A white canvas hat flops from an extended hand or is tossed and falls on the dog's head or sails off to perch in a tree: Bel-Gazou needs no covering other than her chestnut hair, cut straight above her brows and at the nape.

> Oh-what-mis-er-y!
> Oh-what-mis-er-y!

She bounds off, a blaze of red and white in her striped sailor's jersey, and dives into the house, suddenly swallowed by the shadows.

Noon. A midday without a cloud or a breeze, a midday that swells the worm-eaten woodwork, fades the rose twining among the iron grillework at the window, settles down the birds. Sunlight stabs the library from one wall to the other and nails on one panel the horned shadow of an araucaria tree. The bees nesting in the wall are working with innocent frenzy and weave a thread of gold as they fly about the room, thudding against a window, plundering the pink foxglove standing in a tall vase, whipping against my cheek and against Bel-Gazou's cheek, but without stinging anyone at all.

Until seven o'clock, the summer day will triumph over the thickness of the walls, the depth of the oblique embrasures. In declining, the sun will transform the plates hanging on the wall into so many mirrors to reflect his glory. But after seven o'clock the sun will leave this big piece of open sky stretched in front of us and will fall behind the poplars at first, then behind a tower . . . We will pull some furniture out on the balcony—the reading table, the armchair, and Bel-Gazou's campstool—and I will count on another good hour, still, of daylight. When a coolness rises from the valley, barely perceptible at first, felt only by the nostrils and the lips, ignored by the coarse surfaces of the skin, I will raise my head, astonished to find the page of the book that was pink a while ago in the sunset light is now turning periwinkle blue.

It shall not yet be night, no, no, not yet!

Colette, My Mother's House, 1922

🐝 Those who in July are wed, must labour for their daily bread.

Selborne, July 8, 1773

Some young men went down lately to a pond on the verge of Wolmer-forest to hunt flappers, or young wild-ducks, many of which they caught, and, among the rest, some very minute yet well-fledged wild-fowls alive, which, upon examination, I found to be teals. I did not know till then that teals ever bred in the south of England, and was much pleased with the discovery: this I look upon as a great stroke in natural history.

We have had, ever since I can remember, a pair of white owls that constantly breed under the eaves of this church. As I have paid good attention to the manner of life of these birds during their season of breeding, which lasts the summer through, the following remarks may not perhaps be unacceptable: About an hour before sunset (for then the mice begin to run) they sally forth in quest of prey, and hunt all round the hedges of meadows and small enclosures for them, which seem to be their only food. In this irregular country we can stand on an eminence and see them beat the fields over like a setting-dog, and often drop down in the grass or corn. I have minuted these birds with my watch for an hour together, and have found that they return to their nests, the one or the other of them, about once in five minutes; reflecting at the same time on the adroitness that every animal is possessed of as regards the well-being of itself and offspring. But a piece of address, which they show when they return loaded, should not, I think, be passed over in silence.—As they take their prey with their claws, so they carry it in their claws to their nest: but, as the feet are necessary in their ascent under the tiles, they constantly perch first on the roof of the chancel, and shift the mouse from their claws to their bill, that the feet may be at liberty to take hold of the plate on the wall as they are rising under the eaves.

White owls seem not (but in this I am not positive) to hoot at all: all that clamorous hooting appears to me to come from the wood kinds. The white owl does indeed snore and hiss in a tremendous manner; and these menaces will answer the intention of intimidating: for I have known a whole village up in arms on such an occasion, imagining the church-yard to be full of goblins and spectres. White owls also often scream horribly as they fly along; from this screaming probably arose the common people's imaginary species of screech-owl, which they superstitiously think attends the windows of dying persons. The plumage of the remiges of the wings of every species of owl that I have yet examined is remarkably soft and pliant. Perhaps it may be necessary that the wings of these birds should not make much resistance or rushing, that they may be enabled to steal through the air unheard upon a nimble and watchful quarry.

Gilbert White, *The Natural History of Selborne*, 1789

To awake as the summer sun came slanting over hill-tops, with hope on every beam a-dance to the laughter of the morning; to see the leaves across the window ruffling on the fresh new air, and the tendrils of the powdery vine turning from their beaded sleep. Then the lustrous meadows far beyond the thatch of the garden wall, yet seen beneath the hanging scollops of the walnut tree, all awaking, dressed in pearl, all amazed at their own glistening, like a maid at her own ideas. Down them troop the lowing kine, walking each with a step of character (even as men and women do), yet all alike with toss of horns, and spread of udders ready. From them, without a word, we turn to the farmyard proper, seen on the right, and dryly strawed from the petty rush of the pitch-paved runnel. Round it stand the snug outbuildings, barn, corn-chamber, cider-press, stables, with a blinkered horse in every doorway munching, while his driver tightens buckles, whistles and looks down the lane, dallying to begin his labour till the milk-maids be gone by. Here the cock comes forth at last;—where has he been lingering? he claps his wings and shouts 'cock-a-doodle'. But while the cock is crowing still, and the pullet world admiring him, who comes up but the old turkey-cock with all his family round him? Then the geese at the lower end begin to thrust their breasts out, and mum their down-bits, and look at the gander, and scream shrill joy for the conflict; while the ducks in pond show nothing but tail, in proof of their strict neutrality.

While yet we dread for the coming event, and the fight which would jar on the morning, behold the grandmother of sows, gruffly grunting, right and left, with muzzle which no ring can tame (not being matrimonial), hulks across between the two, moving all each side at once, and then all of the other side, as if she were chined down the middle, and afraid of spilling the salt from her. As this mighty view of lard hides each combatant from the other, gladly each retires, and boasts how he would have slain his neighbour, but that old sow drove the other away, and no wonder he was afraid of her, after all the chicks she has eaten.

And so it goes on; and so the sun comes, stronger from his drink of dew; and the cattle in the byres, and the horses from the stable, and the men from the cottage-door, each has had his rest and food, all smell alike of hay and straw, and every one must hie to work, be it drag, or draw, or delve.

Richard Blackmore, *Lorna Doone*, 1869

July is named after Julius Caesar, the dictator of Rome, who was born in the seventh month, and who invaded Britain in 55 BC.

The 15 July is St Swithin's Day.

> St Swithin's Day, if thou dost rain,
> For forty days it will remain.
> St Swithin's Day, if thou be fair,
> For forty days t'will rain nae mair.

St Swithin was Bishop of Winchester in the ninth century. He was a kind and humble man. When he died he asked to be buried outside his church so that his grave would be trodden on by the feet of passers-by, and would receive the raindrops from the eaves. The story is that when the monks wished to move his body many years later, it rained so hard for forty days that they gave up the idea.

The ceremony of swan-upping takes place in July. The swan-markers (wearing special uniforms) row up the Thames from London Bridge to Henley, collecting all the swans and marking the beaks of the cygnets.

Septima, *Something to Do*, 1966

On Tuesday, July 26 [1763], I found Mr Johnson alone. It was a very wet day, and I again complained of the disagreeable effects of such weather. JOHNSON. 'Sir, this is all imagination, which physicians encourage; for man lives in air, as a fish lives in water; so that if the atmosphere press heavy from above, there is an equal resistance from below. To be sure, bad weather is hard upon people who are obliged to be abroad; and men cannot labour so well in the open air in bad weather, as in good: but, Sir, a smith or taylor, whose work is within doors, will surely do as much in rainy weather, as in fair. Some very delicate frames, indeed, may be affected by wet weather; but not common constitutions.'

Boswell's *Life of Johnson*, 1791

Summer Rain

Thick lay the dust, uncomfortably white,
In glaring mimicry of Arab sand.
The woods and mountains slept in hazy light;
The meadows look'd athirst and tawny tanned;
The little rills had left their channels bare,
With scarce a pool to witness what they were;
And the shrunk river gleamed 'mid oozy stones,
That stared like any famished giant's bones.

81

Sudden the hills grew black, and hot as stove
The air beneath; it was a toil to be.
There was a growling as of angry Jove,
Provoked by Juno's prying jealousy—
A flash—a crash—the firmament was split,
And down it came in drops—the smallest fit
To drown a bee in fox-glove bell conceal'd;
Joy filled the brook, and comfort cheered the field.

Hartley Coleridge, 1851

Not one of the sun's numerous admirers had courage to look him in the face: there was no bearing the world till he had said 'Good-night' to it. Then we might stir: then we began to wake and to live. All day long we languished under his influence in a strange dreaminess, too hot to work, too hot to read, too hot to write, too hot even to talk; sitting hour after hour in a green arbour, embowered in leafiness, letting thought and fancy float as they would. Those day-dreams were pretty things in their way; there is no denying that. But then, if one half of the world were to dream through a whole summer, like the sleeping Beauty in the wood, what would become of the other?

The only office requiring the slightest exertion, which I performed in that warm weather, was watering my flowers. Common sympathy called for that labour. The poor things withered, and faded, and pined away; they almost, so to say, panted for draught. Moreover, if I had not watered them myself, I suspect that no one else would; for water last year was nearly as precious hereabout as wine. Our land-springs were dried up; our wells were exhausted; our deep ponds were dwindling into mud; and geese, and ducks, and pigs, and laundresses, used to look with a jealous and suspicious eye on the few and scanty half-buckets of that impure element, which my trusty lacquey was fain to filch for my poor geraniums and campanulas and tuberoses.

Mary Russell Mitford, *Our Village*, 1824–32

By ten o'clock the heat was really on—often the thermometer was hovering about the 90-degree mark. By lunchtime the sweltering atmosphere was almost intolerable. It was so totally unlike Britain; the air seemed completely lifeless. There was no breeze, nothing stirred, grass plants and trees drooped in defeat. We wondered if anything would survive it for long.

Even in the evenings there was no respite from the heat. It was as if the ground had become so hot during the day that it radiated heat long after the sun went down. Only in the still hours before dawn was there a refreshing coolness in the air. Tom and I particularly missed our normal evening walks round the farm. The days seemed long gone when we had strolled in the lingering summer dusk checking the stock, fences and water troughs and discussing plans for the future.

The heat affected everyone and everything. The house was plagued by flies which seemed quite undaunted by the strings of fly-killing strips decorating the kitchen. I was reluctant to gas the lot with an aerosol because the baby was at the vacuum-cleaning stage. Every piece of straw and scrap of fluff on the floor went straight into his mouth. Meals were like a magician's turn with food thrown onto the table and then whipped off again, before the flies could get busy.

Wood warped and metal joints loosened as the temperatures went on soaring. We still had a drop of water left in the well but the pump on it caused endless trouble because the joints in the pipes had expanded and let in air. Gates and wooden fencing collapsed with heat exhaustion. To make matters worse, when we first went to mend them the heads of the hammers flew off. From then on tools with wooden handles were kept in a bucket of water.

The backs of the kitchen chairs rattled and the bars of the baby's playpen become so loose that one day he made a bid for freedom and got his head stuck between them. It was not long before our tempers became as warped as the wood.

The first of July marked the start of our water buying and begging activities. We decided we could not risk any longer trying to get by on our own resources. We would have to look further afield for water. The pond had dried up completely. All the rainwater tanks were empty. I rang the Water Authority and asked for a tankerful. Other people were obviously in the same predicament because it took us over half an hour to get through to the Water Board—all the telephone lines were busy from 8.30 a.m. The authority officials were helpful, and promised a load that afternoon.

Our first sight of the tanker rather stunned us. We had no idea of the quantity of water our cattle drank until we saw the tank sitting there on the back of a flatbed lorry. It was a great gleaming vehicle, remarkably clean after its trip up our dusty drive. The cylindrical tank looked enormous. It proved however to contain only 1000 gallons of water which barely half-filled our cisterns.

The whole operation was remarkably like a fire-fighting exercise. The driver backed up to the barn, leapt out of his cab and unrolled a long canvas hose-pipe. With this he scaled the ladder to the cisterns in the loft, shoved the end at Tom and disappeared back to the lorry. There was a sound of revving up and the water started to gush into the tanks. It shot out under great pressure and we had to struggle to keep the hose-pipe in the right direction. After months of seeing that precious commodity dribble out of almost empty taps we could hardly believe our eyes—there was so much of it all at once. But within a few minutes the tanks were half-full and the tanker was empty.

The driver rolled up the hose-pipe and emptied the dregs into a bucket. 'No sense wasting any. Not when you're paying the price you are,' he remarked cheerfully. We offered him a cup of tea.

'No thanks. You pay mainly on distance and time. It would cost you a fortune, mate. Besides I've another three loads to deliver this morning. Lots of people are out of water, I'm delivering all over the county.'

Evelyn Cox, *The Great Drought of 1976*, 1978

Hymn to the Sun

'Voy wawm' said the dustman
one bright August morning—
But that was in Longbenton,
under the trees.

He was Northumbrian, he'd never known
horizons shimmering in the sun,
men with swart noontide faces sleeping, thick with flies,
by roadside cherry trees.

He was Northumbrian, how should he know
mirage among blue hills,
thin streams that tinkle silence in the still
pulsating drone of summer—

How should he know
how cool the darkness in the white-washed inns
after the white road dancing, and the stones,
and quick dry lizards, round Millevaches?

'*Fait chaud*,' as each old woman said,
going over the hill, in Périgord,
prim in tight bonnets, worn black dresses, and content
with the lilt of sunlight in their bones.

Michael Roberts, 1930

Thus one couple after another with much the same irregular and aimless movement passed the flower-bed and were enveloped in layer after layer of green blue vapour, in which at first their bodies had substance and a dash of colour, but later both substance and colour dissolved in the green-blue atmosphere. How hot it was! So hot that even the thrush chose to hop, like a mechanical bird, in the shadow of the flowers, with long pauses between one movement and the next; instead of rambling vaguely the white butterflies danced one above another, making with their white shifting flakes the outline of a shattered marble column above the tallest flowers; the glass roofs of the palm house shone as if a whole market full of shiny green umbrellas had opened in the sun; and in the drone of the aeroplane the voice of the summer sky murmured its fierce soul. Yellow and black, pink and snow white, shapes of all these colours, men, women, and children were spotted for a second upon the horizon, and then, seeing the breadth of yellow that lay upon the grass, they wavered and sought shade beneath the trees, dissolving like drops of water in the yellow and green atmosphere, staining it faintly with red and blue. It seemed as if all gross and heavy bodies had sunk down in the heat motionless and lay huddled upon the ground, but their voices went wavering from them as if they were flames lolling from the thick waxen bodies of candles. Voices. Yes, voices. Wordless voices, breaking the silence suddenly with such depth of contentment, such passion of desire, or, in the voices of children, such freshness of surprise; breaking the silence? But there was no silence; all the time the motor-omnibuses were turning their wheels and changing their gear; like a vast nest of Chinese boxes all of wrought steel turning ceaselessly one within

another the city murmured; on the top of which the voices cried aloud
and the petals of myriads of flowers flashed their colours into the air.

Virginia Woolf, *Kew Gardens*, 1927

Work and Play

The swallow of summer, she toils all summer,
A blue-dark knot of glittering voltage,
A whiplash swimmer, a fish of the air.
    But the serpent of cars that crawls through the dust
    In shimmering exhaust
    Searching to slake
    Its fever in ocean
    Will play and be idle or else it will bust.

The swallow of summer, the barbed harpoon,
She flings from the furnace, a rainbow of purples,
Dips her glow in the pond and is perfect.
    But the serpent of cars that collapsed at the beach
    Disgorges its organs
    A scamper of colours
    Which roll like tomatoes
    Nude as tomatoes
    With sand in their creases
    To cringe in the sparkle of rollers and screech.

The swallow of summer, the seamstress of summer,
She scissors the blue into shapes and she sews it,
She draws a long thread and she knots it at corners.
    But the holiday people
    Are laid out like wounded
    Flat as in ovens
    Roasting and basting
    With faces of torment as space burns them blue
    Their heads are transistors
    Their teeth grit on sand grains
    Their lost kids are squalling
    While man-eating flies
    Jab electric shock needles but what can they do?

They can climb in their cars with raw bodies, raw faces
    And start up the serpent
    And headache it homeward
    A car full of squabbles
    And sobbing and stickiness
    With sand in their crannies
    Inhaling petroleum
    That pours from the foxgloves
    While the evening swallow
The swallow of summer, cartwheeling through crimson,
Touches the honey-slow river and turning
Returns to the hand stretched from under the eaves—
A boomerang of rejoicing shadow.

                         Ted Hughes, *Season Songs*, 1976

On Saturday morning, August 4, 1921, at a quarter past five, Horace Cairie woke up and heard the rustle of wind in the trees outside his bedroom window. Or was it a gentle, steady rain pattering on the leaves? Oh, no, it couldn't be! That would be too rotten. Red sky at night shepherd's delight. And the sky last night had been red as a great rose and redder, simply crimson. 'Now mind, if you over-excite yourself and don't get proper sleep, you won't be able to enjoy the match or anything!' his mother had said, and Horace knew that what she said was true. Still, what was a fellow to do? Turn over and go to sleep? If it rained, it rained, and there was an end of it: his getting up to see whether the pattery, rustly sound was the wind or rain would not alter the weather. For a chap of fifteen and a few months he feared that he was an awful kid.

He got out of bed deliberately as any man and walked to the window. He leaned out as far as he could lean and surveyed the morning sky with the solemnity of an expert.

Not a cloud was to be seen anywhere; only a breath of wind sufficient to rustle a few dried ivy leaves against the window-sill. A delicate haze spread over the country to the hills.

What a day it would be to watch a cricket match, and suppose Joe Furze couldn't turn out and he were asked to play! And suppose, when he went in to bat five runs were wanted and he got a full toss to leg and hit it plumb right for a four and then with a little luck . . . or supposing Tillingford had batted first and the others wanted six runs and he had a great high catch and held it or a real fast one and jumped out and it stuck in his fingers. Oh, goodness, what a clinking game cricket was!

Hugh de Selincourt, *The Cricket Match*, 1924

August Bank Holiday. A tune on an ice-cream cornet. A slap of sea and a tickle of sand. A fanfare of sunshades opening. A wince and whinny of bathers dancing into deceptive water. A tuck of dresses. A rolling of trousers. A compromise of paddlers. A sunburn of girls and a lark of boys. A silent hullabaloo of balloons.

I remember the sea telling lies in a shell held to my ear for a whole harmonious, hollow minute by a small, wet girl in an enormous bathing-suit marked 'Corporation Property.'

I remember sharing the last of my moist buns with a boy and a lion. Tawny and savage, with cruel nails and capacious mouth, the little boy tore and devoured. Wild as seed-cake, ferocious as a hearth-rug, the depressed and verminous lion nibbled like a mouse at his half a bun, and hiccupped in the sad dusk of his cage.

I remember a man like an alderman or a bailiff, bowlered and collarless, with a bag of monkey-nuts in his hand, crying 'Ride 'em, cowboy!' time and again as he whirled in his chairoplane giddily above the upturned laughing faces of the town girls bold as brass and the boys with padded shoulders and shoes sharp as knives; and the monkey-nuts flew through the air like salty hail.

Children all day capered or squealed by the glazed or bashing sea, and the steam-organ wheezed its waltzes in the threadbare playground and the waste lot, where the dodgems dodged, behind the pickle factory.

And mothers loudly warned their proud pink daughters or sons to put that jellyfish down; and fathers spread newspapers over their faces; and sand-fleas hopped on the picnic lettuce; and someone had forgotten the salt.

In those always radiant, rainless, lazily rowdy and sky-blue summers departed, I remember August Monday from the rising of the sun over the stained and royal town to the husky hushing of the round-about music and the dowsing of the naphtha jets in the seaside fair: from bubble-and-squeak to the last of the sandy sandwiches. . . .

This was the morning when father, mending one hole in the thermos-flask, made three; when the sun declared war on the butter, and the butter ran; when dogs, with all the sweet-binned backyards to wag and sniff and bicker in, chased their tails in the jostling kitchen, worried sandshoes, snapped at flies, writhed between legs, scratched among towels, sat smiling on hampers. . . .

There was cricket on the sand, and sand in the sponge cake, sand-flies in the watercress, and foolish, mulish, religious donkeys on the unwilling trot. Girls undressed in slipping tents of propriety; under invisible umbrellas, stout ladies dressed for the male and immoral sea. Little naked navvies dug canals; children with spades and no ambition built fleeting castles; wispy young men, outside the bathing-huts, whistled at substantial young women and dogs who desired thrown stones more than the bones of elephants. Recalcitrant uncles huddled over luke ale in the tiger-striped marquees. Mothers in black, like wobbling mountains, gasped under the discarded dresses of daughters who shrilly braved the goblin waves. And fathers, in the once-a-year sun, took fifty winks. Oh, think of all the fifty winks along the paper-bagged sand.

Liquorice allsorts, and Welsh hearts, were melting, and the sticks of rock, that we all sucked, were like barbers' poles made of rhubarb.

In the distance, surrounded by disappointed theoreticians and an ironmonger with a drum, a cross man on an orange-box shouted that holidays were wrong.

And the waves rolled in, with rubber ducks and clerks upon them.

I remember the patient, laborious, and enamouring hobby, or profession, of burying relatives in sand.

I remember the princely pastime of pouring sand, from cupped hands or buckets, down collars and tops of dresses; the shriek, the shake, the slap.

I can remember the boy by himself, the beachcombing lone-wolf, hungrily waiting at the edge of family cricket; the friendless fielder, the boy uninvited to bat or to tea.

I remember the smell of sea and seaweed, wet flesh, wet hair, wet bathing-dresses, the warm smell as of a rabbity field after rain, the smell of pop and splashed sunshades and toffee, the stable-and-straw smell of hot, tossed, tumbled, dug, and trodden sand, the swill-and-gaslamp smell of Saturday night, though the sun shone strong, from the bellying beer-tents, the smell of the vinegar on shelled cockles, winkle-smell, shrimp-smell, the dripping-oily backstreet winter-smell of chips in newspapers, the smell of ships from the sun-dazed docks round the corner of the sand-hills, the smell of the known and paddled-in sea moving, full of the drowned and herrings, out and away and beyond and further still towards the antipodes that hung their koala-bears and Maoris, kangaroos, and boomerangs, upside down over the backs of the stars.

And the noise of pummelling Punch, and Judy falling, and a clock tolling or telling no time in the tenantless town; now and again a bell from a lost tower or a train on the lines behind us clearing its throat, and always the hopeless, ravenous swearing and pleading of the gulls, donkey-bray and hawker-cry, harmonicas and toy trumpets, shouting and laughing and singing, hooting of tugs and tramps, the clip of the chair-attendant's puncher, the motor-boat coughing in the bay, and the same hymn and washing of the sea that was heard in the Bible.

'If it could only just, if it could only just?' your lips said again and again as you scooped, in the hob-hot sand, dungeons, garages, torture-chambers, train tunnels, arsenals, hangars for zeppelins, witches' kitchens, vampires' parlours, smugglers' cellars, trolls' grog-shops, sewers, under a ponderous and cracking castle, 'If it could only just be like this for ever and ever amen.'

Dylan Thomas, Quite Early One Morning, 1954

A South Coast Idyll

Beneath these sun-warm'd pines among the heather,
A white goat, bleating, strains his hempen tether,
   A purple stain dreams on the broad blue plain,
The waters and the west wind sing together.

The soft grey lichen creeps o'er ridge and hollow,
Where swift and sudden skims the slim sea swallow;
   The hid cicalas play their viols all the day,
Merry of heart, although they may not follow.

Beyond yon slope, out-wearied with his reaping,
With vine-bound brows, young Daphnis lies a-sleeping;
   Stolen from the sea on feet of ivory,
The white nymphs whisper, through the pine stems peeping.

We hear their steps, yet turn to seek them never,
Nor scale the sunny slope in fond endeavour;
    It may not be, too swiftly would they flee
Our world-stain'd gaze and come no more for ever.

Pan, Pan is piping in the noontide golden,
Let us lie still, as in a dream enfolden,
    Hear by the sea the airs of Arcady,
And feel the wind of tresses unbeholden.

                              Rosamund Marriott Watson

Laughing Song

When the green woods laugh with the voice of joy,
And the dimpling stream runs laughing by;
When the air does laugh with our merry wit,
And the green hill laughs with the noise of it;

When the meadows laugh with lively green,
And the grasshopper laughs in the merry scene;
When Mary and Susan and Emily
With their sweet round mouths sing 'Ha, Ha, He!'

When the painted birds laugh in the shade,
Where our table with cherries and nuts is spread:
Come live, and be merry, and join with me,
To sing the sweet chorus of 'Ha, Ha, He!'

                    William Blake, *Songs of Innocence*, 1789

We Lying by Seasand

We lying by seasand, watching yellow
And the grave sea, mock who deride
Who follow the red rivers, hollow
Alcove of words out of cicada shade,
For in this yellow grave of sand and sea
A calling for colour calls with the wind

That's grave and gay as grave and sea
Sleeping on either hand.
The lunar silences, the silent tide
Lapping the still canals, the dry tide-master
Ribbed between desert and water storm,
Should cure our ills of the water
With a one-coloured calm;
The heavenly music over the sand
Sounds with the grains as they hurry
Hiding the golden mountains and mansions
Of the grave, gay seaside land.
Bound by a sovereign strip, we lie,
Watch yellow, wish for wind to blow away
The strata of the shore and leave red rock;
But wishes breed not, neither
Can we fend off the rock arrival,
Lie watching yellow until the golden weather
Breaks, O my heart's blood, like a heart and hill.

Dylan Thomas, 1952

There are only two ways of eating strawberries. One is neat in the strawberry bed, and the other is mashed on the plate. The first method generally requires us to take up a bent position under a net—in a hot sun very uncomfortable, and at any time fatal to the hair. The second method takes us into the privacy of the home, for it demands a dressing-gown and no spectators. For these reasons I think the strawberry an overrated fruit. Yet I must say that I like to see one floating in cider cup. It gives a note of richness to the affair, and excuses any shortcomings in the lunch itself.

Raspberries are a good fruit gone wrong. A raspberry by itself might indeed be the best fruit of all; but it is almost impossible to find it alone. I do not refer to its attachment to the red currant; rather to the attachment to it of so many of our dumb little friends. The instinct of the lower creatures for the best is well shown in the case of the raspberry. If it is to be eaten it must be picked by the hand, well shaken, and then taken.

When you engage a gardener, the first thing to do is to come to an understanding with him about the peaches. The best way of settling the matter is to give him the carrots and the black currants and the rhubarb for himself, to allow him a free hand with the groundsel and the walnut trees, and to insist in return for this that you should pick the peaches when and how you like. If he is a gentleman he will consent. Supposing that some satisfactory arrangement were come to, and supposing also that you had a silver-bladed pocket-knife with which you could peel them in the open air, then peaches would come very high in the list of fruits. But the conditions are difficult.

Gooseberries burst at the wrong end and smother you; melons . . . make your ears sticky; currants, when you have removed the skin and extracted the seeds, are unsatisfying; blackberries have the faults of raspberries without their virtues; plums are never ripe. Yet all these fruits are excellent in their season. Their faults are faults which we can forgive during a slight acquaintance, which indeed seem but pleasant little idiosyncrasies in the stranger. But we could not live with them.

A. A. Milne, 'Golden Fruit', Not that it Matters

For the height of summer the well-known cold sweet, Summer Pudding, was made from any fruit that was ripe. So we had it made from red currants when the red berries were translucent, gleaming by the garden wall, of black currants when the strings of black juicy berries covered the trees by the white rose, or of raspberries. The best loved was the summer pudding made from the wild bilberries growing in Bilberry Wood on the top of a hill. We set off on a summer afternoon with little tin cans and a basket containing a bottle of milk, and china mugs, and cakes for a picnic tea.

Bilberry Wood was an enchanted place. There lived a fox and rabbits, many birds and lovely trees. The mountain ash and silver birch added to the lightness of the air. There were no dense frightening places in this wood. All was light and air, so heather grew in the sunny spaces and bilberry bushes made little round springy cushions where we sat for tea. When the berries were ripe we sat on the projecting black stones and picked the blue-black berries which we threaded on stalks of fine grass. We came home with blue-black mouths and fingers, for we ate nearly as much as we gathered. The bilberries growing in that wood, and in the lane under the dark walls, were so fresh that each had a bloom on its skin, and we picked the fruit trying not to harm this delicate painting by nature. The bloom on fruit always interested us, and we were careful with the Victoria plums, the damsons and the apples, regarding the bloom as something mysterious, like lace on a dress, or a feather on a bird, a decoration not made by man.

Summer Pudding

The fruit is simmered with sugar until soft. Then a basin is lined closely with strips of bread. The pieces must make a close-knit mould inside the bowl, with no cracks. Into this pour the hot fruit and enough of the juice to keep the fruit fairly stiff and to saturate the bread. Cover the top with a lid of bread, using no crusts. Finally place a saucer on the top with a heavy weight—two or three pounds. Leave the pudding all night in a cold place, for the juice to permeate the bread, and the whole pudding to congeal to firmness. The next day carefully turn it out and serve with thick cream or egg custard.

Alison Uttley, *Recipes from an Old Farmhouse*, 1973

> Fruit gathered too timely will taste of the wood,
>   will shrink and be bitter, and seldom prove good.
> So fruit that is shaken, or beat off a tree,
>   with bruising in falling, soon faulty will be.

Anon.

I have found only two satisfying places in the world in August—the Bodleian Library and a little reedy, willowy pond, where you may enjoy the month perfectly, sitting and being friendly with moorhen and kingfisher and snake, except in the slowly recurring intervals when you catch a tench and cast only mildly envious eyes upon its cool, olive sides. Through the willows I see the hot air quiver in crystal ripples like the points of swords, and sometimes I see a crimson cyclist on a gate. This is 'fantastic summer's heat' divine. For in August it is right to be cool and at the same time to enjoy the sight and perfume of heat out of doors. In June and July the frosts and east winds of May are so near in memory that they give a satisfaction to the sensation of heat. In September frosts and east winds return. August, in short, is the month of Nature's perfect poise, and I should like to see it represented in painting by a Junoesque woman, immobile, passionless, and happy in a cool-leaved wood, and looking neither forward nor backward, but within.

Far off I see a forest-covered hill that says 'Peace' with a great, quiet voice. From the pool and towards the hill runs a shining road, with some of its curves visible for miles, which I have not followed and dare not follow, because it seems to lead to the Happy Fields.

Between the pool and the road is a house built squarely of white stone. A tiled roof, where the light is always mellow as sunset in the various hues that sometimes mix and make old gold, slopes from the many-angled chimneys and juts out beyond and below the wall of the house. In that shadowy pocket of the eaves the martins build, and on a day of diamond air their shadows are as rivulets upon the white wall. Four large windows frame a cool and velvety and impenetrable gloom. Between them stand four still cypresses.

A footpath skirts the pool and on one side tall grasses rise up, on the other thorns and still more grasses, heavy with flowers and the weight of birds. The grasses almost meet across the path, and a little way ahead mix in a mist through which the white-throat and the dragon-fly climb or descend continually. The little green worlds below the meeting grasses are full of the music of bright insects and the glow of flowers. The long stems ascend in the most perfect grace; pale green, cool, and pleasant to the touch, stately and apparently full of strength, with a certain benignity of shape that is pleasant to the eye and mind. Branched, feathered, and tufted heads of flowers top the tall grass, and in the clear air each filament divides itself from the rest as the locks of the river-moss divide on the water's flow. All bend in trembling curves with their own fullness, and the butterflies crown them from time to time. When wind plays with the perfectly level surface of the grasses their colours close in and part and knit arabesques in the path of the light sand martins. Sometimes the mailed insects creep along the pennons of the grass leaves to sun themselves, other insects visit the forget-me-nots in the pool. Every plant has its miniature dryad.

Edward Thomas, *The Heart of England*, 1906

The sun shines and shines; can this be an English summer? The last spate was in April, and then the river was far from being bank-high. That freshet of coloured water was not even strong enough to dislodge the heaps of brambles which had been cut and thrown into the stream during January. There they still lie, dry and bleached, the old moorhen's nest two feet above the water-level. The willow branches have put out roots, many inches long, into the mass of rotten leaves and wood which has accumulated there.

The usual eddies are motionless and warm, green with algae and flannel weed, and the feeding-place of strange water-beetles. When the spate comes the contents of this and other backwaters will be carried down as pollution. It may kill fish, for it is saturated with carbonic acid gas. Litmus paper dipped into it turns red.

Those salmon and sea-trout which have not been gaffed out by poachers hide themselves marvellously during the daylight. Who would think that a fish thirty-three inches long and ten inches deep could exist, and have existed for six months, in an area of river half as big as a tennis court and varying in depth from two inches to three feet? Every inch of the bottom is lit up in sunlight; search how you will, you will not see the big fish. At dawn the prisoner thrusts himself far under the roots of an alder; you may wade and stroke him, but he will not move in his terror. A white fungus, like that which grows on old timber, has spread over his head and corrupted his tail-fin. He breathes in gulps unevenly.

At twilight, precisely as the bats begin to flitter over the water, the great sea-trout, who came up from the sea in January, sinuates slowly, as though wearily, from his refuge, and hovers awhile near the surface. Sometimes his rusty back-fin idles out. The moon lifts over the spruce firs. The fish turns, pushing a wave as he rips downstream; he rolls like a porpoise, showing a gleam of silver-gold and brown; then he leaps, falling back with a great splash that is heard for a hundred yards and more. He is trying to rid himself of the itch of fungus. Afterwards he hovers again, as he did when he was an ordinary small brown trout years ago; but the itch of maggots in his gills drives him to turn on his side, showing his taper and thickness, and rub head and flank with a flapping movement on the gravel. Afterwards, the listlessness of low warm water comes back to him, and he sinks into a torpor guarded by his senses of sight, hearing, and smell.

On the bank above the pool something moves dimly. It is a sheep, lying on its side. The wasps, seeking meat for their queen grubs, have left it; but the maggots of the blow-flies are working restlessly. This poor beast was treated with a solution of carbolic acid four days ago, but the flies returned to it, and in a short while the ivory-sweaty maggots were again tunnelling between skin and flesh. The shepherd works early and late, but is not so strong as the sun, which must appear as a benevolent god to the flies this year.

The sheep kicks convulsively, and the odours of corruption arise with the damp air moving down from the hills.

Higher up the river there is a delicious smell of honey. For nearly a quarter of a mile one smells it. It is exactly the odour of those yellow beeswax tapers which are burned for the saints in Pyrenean churches. The summer has been kind to bees as well as flies; and many swarms from hive and skep have travelled away and become wild. There are three nests somewhere under the wooden super-structure of the railway viaduct. A patch of oil from a motor car lies beside a patch of honey which has dripped from above. Yesterday I watched a war between one clan and another, for the bees of number one nest raided the honey of number two nest; food is the cause of their war.

The evening star shines over the hill, and the old arrogant cock pheasant has ceased to cry out against the fox peering and sniffing below his roosting fir. It is time to go indoors and light the lamp.

Henry Williamson, 'August Evening', *The Linhay on the Downs*, 1934

Hot Silence

The serpent-rooted pine-trees, row on row
  Just as they stood a thousand years before,
  Rise up innumerable along the shore.
Their glittering cones fleck the white sand below.

The sea is bright with many sails. They look
  As though they had been fastened there in play.
  The green hills on the islands far away
Are small and clear like paintings in a book.

On air and sea there lies a noonday lull:
  Not even a ripple stirs the mirrored sky
  Or wakes the slumbering fish, and not a sigh
Ruffles the smooth back of the flying gull.

Clifford Bax, 75 Chinese Poems, 1910

WEDNESDAY 24TH AUGUST

It is most unlikely now that we shall have the bulk lorry for the grain with the weather as uncertain as this—there is no point in ordering it two days ahead. So when we do harvest it will be into sacks. John went off this morning to buy 300 new ones—they cost 18p each—we stayed under cover of Old Barn mending the used sacks with glue and patches. But at least we have enough now to be getting on with.

No one is looking for ideal harvesting weather now; one dry day and the combine harvester will be able to make a start. That is all we need.

THURSDAY 25TH

The barley is ripe and ready for harvesting. There is at least £3,000-worth of barley standing out there in the fields. Every day's delay now will prove costly. By this time last year the harvest was all done, the grain and straw inside under cover. Each patch of blue in the sky brings fresh hopes that it may be the beginning of a dry spell, but so far we have always been disappointed.

Graham is still having to treat several sheep that have maggots from time to time. Next year if the dipping regulations are the same we will dip in July as well as after the 1st September. The cost of dipping and the work involved is nothing compared to the condition the sheep lose and their suffering with the flies and maggots.

FRIDAY 26TH

There are only four really steep fields on the farm—Brinnen, Ferny Piece, Watercress and Wood Hill. The weed has to be cut on all of them. Graham has already cut Brinnen and today it was Watercress. He cut along the slope at an angle of about 30 degrees; any more and the tractor could have toppled over. It had to be done slowly and carefully, for once a tractor starts to turn over there's little the driver can do. For this we always use the big tractor with the safety cab. It took Graham most of the day to finish Watercress; and there are still a few yards near the hedge at the top where it's too steep to cut except by hand.

David spring-cleaned the dairy and began repainting the walls where the paint has flaked badly.

Michael Morpurgo, *All Around the Year*, 1979

London Summer

My window lays its grid on the map of a sky
Charted with molten islands; and the sun
Sails mythically into the towered west
Till London is Athens, Valparaiso, Rome.
Steeple and dome,
Which, in the heat of noon,
Wavered as though submerged, float on the last
Sea-green tide of a day's end, and die.

 Now the weaving lights appear
 From pavement, tree and parapet
 Till the drowsy eyes forget
 Which, in the Sicilian air,
 Is firefly, star and cigarette.

Browner than bracken, the barefoot corner-boys
Lean over green grapes bubbling on a barrow
And watermelons, plucked where the whip-poor-will
Whined all night like a hawker about my home.
Summer has come
And will be here tomorrow
With litter of peel and popcorn, when the still
Sidewalk is brushed again by the morning breeze.

 A Neon moon over World's End
 Is nightfall's first advertisement;
 The ripples on the waterfront
 Lower their Venetian blind;
 The sparrow ceases argument.

Only on the left bank of the east river
(The Liffey, at sunrise, with its paintbox houses;
At night, the Grand Canal whose swans explore
The dark, like gondolas) I hear the shrill
Bat-call
Chatter of young voices
Swarming to the shaft of light at a bar door,
To the honky-tonky piano and the blue-jeaned lover.

> Welter-weight and matelot,
> Ganymede and grenadier
> See, beyond the rendezvous,
> Life forever amber through
> Half a pint of bitter beer.

This City is all cities under the wicked moon,
While summer lasts. Here the Embankment glimmers,
A lemon-grove of lights, at the edge of all
Waters in history; and we, who share
The fabled air
That is a London summer's,
Stretch in a dream our seven-leagued limbs and stroll
A stateless world, where none are alien.

> But O what fancy shall defy
> The nightmare ague in the bone
> When, beneath a winter sky,
> The lost, unearthly cities lie
> Cold and separate as stone?

Paul Dehn, *Romantic Landscape*, 1952

Hurrahing in Harvest

Summer ends now; now, barbarous in beauty, the stooks rise
Around; up above, what wind-walks! what lovely behaviour
Of silk-sack clouds! has wilder, wilful-wavier
Meal-drift moulded ever and melted across skies?

I walk, I lift up, I lift up heart, eyes,
Down all that glory in the heavens to glean our Saviour;
And, éyes, heárt, what looks, what lips yet gave you a
Rapturous love's greeting of realer, of rounder replies?

And the azurous hung hills are his world-wielding shoulder
Majestic—as a stallion stalwart, very-violet-sweet!—
These things, these things were here and but the beholder
Wanting; which two when they once meet,
The heart rears wings bold and bolder
And hurls for him, O half hurls earth for him off under his feet.

Gerard Manley Hopkins, 1877

♣ Dry August and warm, does harvest no harm.

Go, for they call you, Shepherd, from the hill;
    Go, Shepherd, and untie the wattled cotes:
        No longer leave thy wistful flock unfed,
    Nor let thy bawling fellows rack their throats,
        Nor the cropp'd grasses shoot another head.
            But when the fields are still,
    And the tired men and dogs all gone to rest,
        And only the white sheep are sometimes seen
        Cross and recross the strips of moon-blanch'd green;
            Come, Shepherd, and again renew the quest.

Here, where the reaper was at work of late,
    In this high field's dark corner, where he leaves
        His coat, his basket, and his earthen cruise,
    And in the sun all morning binds the sheaves,
        Then here, at noon, comes back his stores to use;
            Here will I sit and wait,
    While to my ear from uplands far away
        The bleating of the folded flocks is borne,
        With distant cries of reapers in the corn—
            All the live murmur of a summer's day.

Screen'd in this nook o'er the high, half-reap'd field,
And here till sun-down, Shepherd, will I be.
Through the thick corn the scarlet poppies peep,
And round green roots and yellowing stalks I see
Pale blue convolvulus in tendrils creep:
And air-swept lindens yield
Their scent, and rustle down their perfum'd showers
Of bloom on the bent grass where I am laid,
And bower me from the August sun with shade;
And the eye travels down to Oxford's towers . . .

Matthew Arnold, from *The Scholar Gipsy*, 1853

So Many Summers

Beside one loch, a hind's neat skeleton,
Beside another, a boat pulled high and dry:
Two neat geometries drawn in the weather:
Two things already dead and still to die.

I passed them every summer, rod in hand,
Skirting the bright blue or the spitting gray,
And, every summer, saw how the bleached timbers
Gaped wider and the neat ribs fell away.

Time adds one malice to another one—
Now you'd look very close before you knew
If it's the boat that ran, the hind went sailing.
So many summers, and I have lived them too.

Norman MacCaig, *A Man In My Position*, 1969

Exeunt

Piecemeal the summer dies;
At the field's edge a daisy lives alone;
A last shawl of burning lies
On a gray field-stone.

All cries are thin and terse;
The field has droned the summer's final mass;
A cricket like a dwindled hearse
Crawls from the dry grass.

Richard Wilbur, *Poems 1943–1956*, 1957

For some days past, in the mornings, the scents of autumn had been drifting down as far as the sea.

These late August mornings smelt of autumn from daybreak till the hour when the sun-baked earth allowed the cool sea breezes to drive back the then less heavy aroma of threshed wheat, open furrows, and reeking manure. A persistent dew clung sparkling to the skirts of the hedgerows, and if, about noon, Vinca came upon a fallen aspen leaf, the white underside of its still green surface would be damp and glistening. Moist mushrooms poked up through the earth and, now that the nights were chillier, garden spiders retired in the evening to the shed where the playthings were kept, and there wisely took up their abode on the ceiling.

But the midday hours were free of the wisps of autumn mists and of the gossamer threads stretched over bramble bushes laden with blackberries, and the season showed every sign of going back to July. High in the sky the sun sucked up the dew, rotting the morning's mushrooms and smothering with wasps the antiquated vines and their puny clusters. Vinca and Lisette, out walking together, threw off with identical gestures the light woollies that since breakfast had protected their upper arms and bare necks, brown against the white of their frocks. A succession of fine days followed, calm, windless and cloudless except for the milky 'mare's tails' that trailed slowly across the noonday sky only to vanish into thin air: days so divinely akin to each other that Vinca and Philippe, at peace, almost believed the year to be ending at its sweetest moment, softly held in check by an August that would last for ever.

Colette, *Ripening Seed*, 1923

There Came a Day

There came a day that caught the summer
Wrung its neck
Plucked it
And ate it.

Now what shall I do with the trees?
The day said, the day said.
Strip them bare, strip them bare.
Let's see what is really there.

And what shall I do with the sun?
The day said, the day said.
Roll him away till he's cold and small.
He'll come back rested if he comes back at all.

And what shall I do with the birds?
The day said, the day said.
The birds I've frightened, let them flit,
I'll hang out pork for the brave tomtit.

And what shall I do with the seed?
The day said, the day said.
Bury it deep, see what it's worth.
See if it can stand the earth.

What shall I do with the people?
The day said, the day said.
Stuff them with apple and blackberry pie—
They'll love me then till the day they die.

There came this day and he was autumn.
His mouth was wide
And red as a sunset.
His tail was an icicle.

Ted Hughes, *Season Songs*, 1976

AUTUMN

THE long-lasting popularity of Thomson's eighteenth-century didactic poem *The Seasons*, probably served to confirm the fact that to the English mind and sensibility, autumn has become, *par excellence*, the time for 'Philosophic Melancholy': the season when our minds are drawn to thoughts of mortality, and of the ephemeral nature of human joy and delight.

As the leaves fall from the trees and the harvest fields are stripped, so we ourselves—unwittingly echoing Ruskin's 'pathetic fallacy' —shudder diffidently and feel a sense of decline, a falling-off, in our animal spirits.

Autumn, then, is deeply and disturbingly ambivalent: the consummation, through harvest, of all the growth of summer, and simultaneously—and paradoxically—the beginning of the death of the year: a seasonal *post coitum tristis*, a bitter-sweet preface to the rigours of winter, and a resonant reminder of the fact that good things especially, do not last for ever. As for decay, who now reads James Thomson's erstwhile best-seller?

Rich Days

Welcome to you, rich Autumn days,
    Ere comes the cold, leaf-picking wind;
When golden stocks are seen in fields,
    All standing arm-in-arm entwined;
And gallons of sweet cider seen
On trees in apples red and green.

With mellow pears that cheat our teeth,
    Which melt that tongues may suck them in;
With blue-black damsons, yellow plums,
    Now sweet and soft from stone to skin;
And woodnuts rich, to make us go
Into the loneliest lanes we know.

W. H. Davies

To Autumn

O Autumn, laden with fruit, and stainèd
With the blood of the grape, pass not, but sit
Beneath my shady roof; there thou may'st rest,
And tune thy jolly voice to my fresh pipe,
And all the daughters of the year shall dance!
Sing now the lusty song of fruits and flowers.

'The narrow bud opens her beauties to
The sun, and love runs in her thrilling veins;
Blossoms hang round the brows of Morning, and
Flourish down the bright cheek of modest Eve,
Till clust'ring Summer breaks forth into singing,
And feather'd clouds strew flowers round her head.

'The spirits of the air live on the smells
Of fruit; and Joy, with pinions light, roves round
The gardens, or sits singing in the trees.'
Thus sang the jolly Autumn as he sat;
Then rose, girded himself, and o'er the bleak
Hills fled from our sight; but left his golden load.

William Blake, 1783

Now it is the autumn again; the people are all coming back. The recess of summer is over, when holidays are taken, newspapers shrink, history itself seems momentarily to falter and stop. But the papers are thickening and filling again; things seem to be happening; back from Corfu and Sete, Positano and Leningrad, the people are parking their cars and campers in their drives, and opening their diaries, and calling up other people on the telephone. The deckchairs on the beach have been put away, and a weak sun shines on the promenade; there is fresh fighting in Vietnam, while McGovern campaigns ineffectually against Nixon. In the chemists' shops in town, they have removed the sunglasses and the insect-bite lotions, for the summer visitors have left, and have stocked up on sleeping tablets and Librium, the staples of the year-round trade; there is direct rule in Ulster, and a gun-battle has taken place in the Falls Road. The new autumn colours are in the boutiques; there is now on the market a fresh intra-uterine device, reckoned to be ninety-nine per cent safe. Everywhere there are new developments, new indignities; the intelligent people survey the autumn world, and liberal and radical hackles rise, and fresh faces are about, and the sun shines fitfully, and the telephones ring.

Malcolm Bradbury, *The History Man*, 1975

Harrow-on-the-Hill

When melancholy Autumn comes to Wembley
And electric trains are lighted after tea
The poplars near the Stadium are trembly
With their tap and tap and whispering to me,
Like the sound of little breakers
Spreading out along the surf-line
When the estuary's filling
With the sea.

Then Harrow-on-the-Hill's a rocky island
And Harrow churchyard full of sailors' graves
And the constant click and kissing of the trolley buses hissing
Is the level to the Wealdstone turned to waves

And the rumble of the railway
Is the thunder of the rollers
As they gather up for plunging
    Into caves.

There's a storm cloud to the westward over Kenton,
    There's a line of harbour lights at Perivale,
Is it rounding rough Pentire in a flood of sunset fire
    The little fleet of trawlers under sail?
      Can those boats be only roof tops
      As they stream along the skyline
In a race for port and Padstow
    With the gale?

Sir John Betjeman, *A Few Late Chrysanthemums*, 1954

September is the end of summer and the beginning of autumn. Christina Rossetti wrote:

The Spring is like a young maid
That does not know her mind,
The Summer is a tyrant
Of most ungracious kind;
The Autumn is an old friend
That pleases all he can,
And brings the bearded barley
To glad the heart of man.

There are two Saints' days in September, St Matthew on the twenty-first and St Michael the Archangel on the twenty-ninth, so it is a special month for anyone called Matthew or Michael, and also for Marys, because 8 September is the birthday of the Virgin Mary.

Sometimes farmers who could not pay their rents on September quarter day gave their landlord a fat goose to soften his heart and an old rhyme says:

Who so eats goose on Michaelmas Day
Shall never lack money his debts to pay.

Queen Elizabeth is supposed to have been eating goose when, on 29 September 1588, she heard that her navy had defeated the Spanish Armada.   Septima, *Something to Do*, 1966

♣ Marry in September's shine, your living will be rich and fine.

Bavarian Gentians

Not every man has gentians in his house
in soft September, at slow, sad Michaelmas.
Bavarian gentians, tall and dark, but dark
darkening the daytime torch-like with the smoking blueness of
    Pluto's gloom,
ribbed hellish flowers erect, with their blaze of darkness spread blue,
blown flat into points, by the heavy white draught of the day.

Torch-flowers of the blue-smoking darkness, Pluto's dark-blue blaze
black lamps from the halls of Dis, smoking dark blue
giving off darkness, blue darkness, upon Demeter's yellow-pale day
whom have you come for, here in the white-cast day?

Reach me a gentian, give me a torch!
let me guide myself with the blue, forked torch of a flower
down the darker and darker stairs, where blue is darkened on
    blueness
down the way Persephone goes, just now, in first-frosted September,
to the sightless realm where darkness is married to dark
and Persephone herself is but a voice, as a bride,
a gloom invisible enfolded in the deeper dark
of the arms of Pluto as he ravishes her once again
and pierces her once more with his passion of the utter dark
among the splendour of black-blue torches, shedding fathomless
    darkness on the nuptials.

Give me a flower on a tall stem, and three dark flames,
for I will go to the wedding, and be wedding-guest
at the marriage of the living dark.
                  D. H. Lawrence, *Last Poems*, 1932

Autumn

1. Birds seen on holidays. (Pictures)
2. Planting tree seeds.
3. Planting cuttings.
4. Insects.
5. Things to do with seeds and grasses.
6. Autumn leaves.
7. Empty birds' nests.
8. Weed patch.
9. Planting bulbs.
10. Ivy flowers.
11. Toadstool gardens.
12. Newts.
13. Haunts of furry animals. (Pictures)
14. Four-footed creatures without fur. (Pictures)
15. Indoor gardens.
16. Ivy leaves and fir cones.

DETAILS OF AUTUMN WORK

Autumn leaves

As many brought as possible, for enjoyment of colour and rustle.

Ways of using leaves:

(*a*) To fix the bright colours, choose a few of the best and dry in sand. First dry the sand completely for some hours in an oven, or keep by fire or on warm radiator for some days. A shallow baking-tin is suitable. Then put a layer of dry sand, the leaves, and another layer of sand, and keep in a very dry place for quite two weeks. The colours are then set and the leaves can be mounted on card with a touch of gum.

(*b*) To mount for shape, children gather them when fallen and press while still moist between sheets of newspaper (at home if more suitable). Bring leaves to school for lesson, carrying them in their pressing paper. Let small folders be prepared for their reception, or a few of the best chosen for inclusion in the child's personal folder. A big gummed label and pair of scissors for each group will allow for fastening in.

(*c*) Drawing and colouring of leaves. Any way possible; pastel on light brown paper is very effective. A large sheet pinned up, and drawings made by children in turn would be of interest, for the class could suggest what shape and colour would go well on a certain part of the paper.

Empty birds' nests

Birds' nests begin to show clearly as the leaves fall, and there is no harm in taking a few now that their use is over. Explore the materials used. Whose nest is it? Each bird builds in its own way. An empty hedge nest may contain hips, haws, and remains of these. A bank vole or a long-tailed field-mouse has climbed the hedge, gathered the fruit and taken it to the nest; here it gnawed through the pulp to feast on the nutty seeds. E. M. Stephenson, *Nature Study and Rural Science*, A Four Year Course for Juniors, 1966

He comes! he comes! in every breeze the Power
Of Philosophic Melancholy comes!
His near approach the sudden-starting tear,
The glowing cheek, the mild dejected air,
The soften'd feature, and the beating heart,
Pierc'd deep with many a virtuous pang, declare.
O'er all the soul his sacred influence breathes;
Inflames imagination; through the breast
Infuses every tenderness; and far
Beyond dim earth exalts the swelling thought.
Ten thousand thousand fleet ideas, such
As never mingled with the vulgar dream,
Crowd fast into the mind's creative eye.
As fast the correspondent passions rise,
As varied, and as high: Devotion rais'd
To rapture, and divine astonishment;
The love of Nature, unconfin'd, and, chief,
Of human race: the large ambitious wish,
To make them blest; the sigh for suffering worth
Lost in obscurity; the noble scorn

Of tyrant-pride; the fearless great resolve;
The wonder which the dying patriot draws,
Inspiring glory through remotest time;
Th' awaken'd throb for virtue, and for fame;
The sympathies of love, and friendship dear:
With all the social offspring of the heart.

James Thomson, from *The Seasons*, 1726–30

Spring and Fall
to a young child

Márgarét, áre you gríeving
Over Goldengrove unleaving?
Leáves, like the things of man, you
With your fresh thoughts care for, can you?
Áh! ás the heart grows older
It will come to such sights colder
By and by, nor spare a sigh
Though worlds of wanwood leafmeal lie;
And yet you *will* weep and know why.
Now no matter, child, the name:
Sórrow's spríngs áre the same.
Nor mouth had, no nor mind, expressed
What heart heard of, ghost guessed:
It ís the blight man was born for,
It is Margaret you mourn for.

Gerard Manley Hopkins, 1880

Autumn Violets

Keep love for youth, and violets for the spring:
　　Or if these bloom when worn-out autumn grieves
　Let them lie hid in double shade of leaves,
Their own, and others dropped down withering;
For violets suit when home birds build and sing,
　Not when the outbound bird a passage cleaves;
　Not with dry stubble of mown harvest sheaves,

But when the green world buds to blossoming.
Keep violets for the spring, and love for youth,
   Love that should dwell with beauty, mirth, and hope
      Or if a later sadder love be born,
   Let this not look for grace beyond its scope,
But give itself, nor plead for answering truth—
      A grateful Ruth tho' gleaning scanty corn.

Christina Rossetti (1830–94)

Sept. 26 [1873]—Weather has been bright but yesterday was brilliant. Some of our trees make a great gate opening over the park—two poplars for posts; on the left is the tallest of the cedars of more upright, less horizontal/ habit than the others, hive-shaped but set to one side by the wind; then, taller, the poplar beautifully touched with leaf against the sky and below these a tree with a mesh of leaves leaning away, beech and what not; here the break and distant oaks on a height in the park; then the other poplar, more gaunt and part strung and dead, and again other trees lower—Spanish chestnut and Turkey oak. Almost no colour; the cedar laying level crow-feather strokes of boughs, with fine wave and dedication in them, against the light. The sun just above, a shaking white fire or waterball, striking and glanting. Blue of the sky round and below changed to a pale burning flesh. —One of the wychelms in the field between is just shaped in under a branch of a near cedar, its boughs coming and going towards one another in caressed curve and combing

This morning, Sept. 27, blue mist breathing with wind across the garden after mass. Noticed how everything looked less and nearer, not bigger and spacious in the fog. Tops of the trees hidden almost or where seen grey, till the sun threw a moist red light through them. Two beautiful sights: printed upon the sun, a glowing silver piece, came out the sharp visible leafage of invisible trees, on either side nothing whatever could be seen of them, and these leaves handful for handful, changed as I walked; the other was splays of shadow-spokes struck out from any knot of leaves or boughs where the sun was/ like timbers across the thick air

Oct. 17—Woodpigeons come in flock into our field and on our trees: they flock at this time of year

A doe comes to our sunken fence to be fed: she eats acorns and chestnuts and stands on the bank, a pretty triped, forefeet together and hind set apart. The bucks grunt all night at this season and fight often: it is their season

At the end of the month hard frosts. Wonderful downpour of leaf: when the morning sun began to melt the frost they fell at one touch and in a few minutes a whole tree was flung of them; they lay masking and papering the ground at the foot. Then the tree seems to be looking down on its cast self as blue sky on snow after a long fall, its losing, its doing

White poplar leaves at this season silver behind, olive black in front. Birch leaves on a fading tree give three colours, green, white, and yellow   Gerard Manley Hopkins, *Journal*

Reading Outside

The lazy wasps are cruising the lawn, more
savage at the end, their Septembers are
senile, lingering; they fly unfocused,
browse for nothing in the flowerless grass;

they ruffle too easily now, like bullies,
brashly, stumbling over blades; the air
won't hold. We read despite them, warily;
the diminished tigers whine and crawl to

unsettle us with their blundering; even
their absence won't leave us alone, we hurry
with them: impatience is a greed we share.

                                   Adam Phillips, 1979

The autumn is the beginning of the shepherd's year, as you might say. The tups go into the ewes about the first week in September. These aren't the proper tups; they just bring the ewes on. We call them teasers. It means that when you put in the proper tups the ewes are good and ready for them, and can be served in one bunch. Let them love together and they'll lamb together, and that will be convenient. A good ram will serve fifty ewes after the teasers have been with them for a month. I work it like this. I put half my proper tups in with the ewes for two days, then take them out and give them a rest while the other half have a go. Each ram has a harness full of crayon strapped around him, so that when he jumps he marks the ewe. I then know how many ewes are coming. I change the crayon—the raddle—every fifteen days. So the first raddle will be blue, then red. In the olden days they painted the jumped ewes with red ochre but now we have this system of telling. If all the ewes are covered the first fifteen days and none of them come back, then I take the tups out. I leave them roughly three periods to come over—about forty-five days all told.

I usually start lambing in mid-February, although one year I started as early as Christmas Day. It was much too soon. The grass wasn't ready so the lambs had to be kept indoors. The food bills were terrific! I don't have to help a great deal with the births, only be there. This is most important. I never leave the flock then, I am there all the time. I only call the vet if there is a big mishap, such as the womb coming out. I take each lamb away from its mother and do all the little odds and ends like. You can't raise every lamb which is born, there must be some loss. I try and arrange things so that each ewe has two lambs. This shouldn't be difficult if each ewe has been well flushed before the tup services her and has had good pasture. You see, before tupping time the ewes are kept on a bare pasture and then, just a week before the rams are put in, I put them on a high plane of nutrition which is supposed to bring down more ovaries. And so two eggs will come down, and I have had three and even four. I had five sets of quads last year but they were poor little runty things.

I castrate the male lambs, the little tups, about an hour after they have been born. They say that what you've never had, you never miss. I wonder. I do it with rubber rings. It used to be done much later. The tails used to be cut off with a hot iron and the balls nicked out with the shepherd's teeth. He ate well that day. But the tups still go behind a bit after they have been castrated. They get thin. It pulls them down.

It is a surprising thing to happen to you when you have just come into the world on a spring morning. And, of course, I cut the tails off later on—to prevent fly-strike in the summer-time.

Ronald Blythe, *Akenfield: Portrait of an English Village*, 1969

On September the 21st, 1741, being then on a visit, and intent on field-diversions, I rose before daybreak: when I came into the enclosures, I found the stubbles and clover-grounds matted all over with a thick coat of cobweb, in the meshes of which a copious and heavy dew hung so plentifully that the whole face of the country seemed, as it were, covered with two or three setting-nets drawn one over another. When the dogs attempted to hunt, their eyes were so blinded and hoodwinked that they could not proceed, but were obliged to lie down and scrape the incumbrances from their faces with their fore-feet, so that, finding my sport interrupted, I returned home musing in my mind on the oddness of the occurrence.

As the morning advanced the sun became bright and warm, and the day turned out one of those most lovely ones which no season but the autumn produces: cloudless, calm, serene, and worthy of the South of France itself.

About nine an appearance very unusual began to demand our attention, a shower of cobwebs falling from very elevated regions, and continuing, without any interruption, till the close of the day. These webs were not single filmy threads, floating in the air in all directions, but perfect flakes or rags; some near an inch broad, and five or six long, which fell with a degree of velocity which showed they were considerably heavier than the atmosphere.

On every side as the observer turned his eyes might he behold a continual succession of fresh flakes falling into his sight, and twinkling like stars as they turned their sides towards the sun.

How far this wonderful shower extended would be difficult to say; but we know that it reached Bradley, Selborne, and Alresford, three places which lie in a sort of triangle, the shortest of whose sides is about eight miles in extent.

At the second of those places there was a gentleman (for whose veracity and intelligent turn we have the greatest veneration) who observed it the moment he got abroad; but concluded that, as soon as he came upon the hill above his house, where he took his morning rides, he should be higher than this meteor, which he imagined might have been blown, like thistle-down, from the common above: but, to his great astonishment, when he rode to the most elevated part of the down, 300 feet above his fields, he found the webs in appearance still as much above him as before; still descending into sight in a constant succession, and twinkling in the sun, so as to draw the attention of the most incurious.

Neither before nor after was any such fall observed; but on this day the flakes hung in the trees and hedges so thick, that a diligent person sent out might have gathered baskets full.

The remark that I shall make on these cobweb-like appearances, called gossamer, is, that, strange and superstitious as the notions about them were formerly, nobody in these days doubts but that they are the real production of small spiders which swarm in the fields in fine weather in autumn, and have a power of shooting out webs from their tails so as to render themselves buoyant, and lighter than air. But why these apterous insects should that day take such a wonderful aerial excursion, and why their webs should at once become so gross and material as to be considerably more weighty than air, and to descend with precipitation, is a matter beyond my skill. If I might be allowed to hazard a supposition, I should imagine that those filmy threads, when first shot, might be entangled in the rising dew, and so drawn up, spiders and all, by a brisk evaporation into the region where clouds are formed: and if the spiders have a power of coiling and thickening their webs in the air, as Dr Lister says they have, then, when they were become heavier than the air, they must fall.

Every day in fine weather, in autumn chiefly, do I see those spiders shooting out their webs and mounting aloft: they will go off from your finger if you will take them into your hand. Last summer one alighted on my book as I was reading in the parlour; and, running to the top of the page, and shooting out a web, took its departure from thence. But what I most wondered at, was that it went off with considerable velocity in a place where no air was stirring; and I am sure that I did not assist it with my breath. So that these little crawlers seem to have while mounting, some loco-motive power without the use of wings, and to move in the air, faster than the air itself.

Gilbert White, *The Natural History of Selborne*, 1789

Tell me not here, it needs not saying,
　What tune the enchantress plays
In aftermaths of soft September
　Or under blanching mays,
For she and I were long acquainted
　And I knew all her ways.

On russet floors, by waters idle,
　The pine lets fall its cone;
The cuckoo shouts all day at nothing
　In leafy dells alone;
And traveller's joy beguiles in autumn
　Hearts that have lost their own.

On acres of the seeded grasses
　The changing burnish leaves;
Or marshalled under moons of harvest
　Stand still all night the sheaves;
Or beeches strip in storms for winter
　And stain the wind with leaves.

Possess, as I possessed a season,
　The countries I resign,
Where over elmy plains the highway
　Would mount the hills and shine,
And full of shade the pillared forest
　Would murmur and be mine.

For nature, heartless, witless nature,
　Will neither care nor know
What stranger's feet may find the meadow
　And trespass there and go,
Nor ask amid the dews of morning
　If they are mine or no.

A. E. Housman

In Autumn when the woods are red
And skies are grey and clear,
The sportsmen seek the wild fowls' bed
Or follow down the deer;
And Cupid hunts by haugh and head,
By riverside and mere,
I walk, not seeing where I tread
And keep my heart with fear,
Sir, have an eye, on where you tread,
And keep your heart with fear,
For something lingers here;
A touch of April not yet dead,
In Autumn when the woods are red
And skies are grey and clear.

Robert Louis Stevenson, 1882

The Cow in Apple Time

Something inspires the only cow of late
To make no more of a wall than an open gate,
And think no more of wall-builders than fools.
Her face is flecked with pomace and she drools
A cider syrup. Having tasted fruit,
She scorns a pasture withering to the root.
She runs from tree to tree where lie and sweeten
The windfalls spiked with stubble and worm-eaten.
She leaves them bitten when she has to fly.
She bellows on a knoll against the sky.
Her udder shrivels and the milk goes dry.

Robert Frost

The last village was far behind. The last happy chapel-goer has passed me long ago. A cock crowed once and said the last word on repose. The rain fell gently; the stems of the hazels in the thickets gleamed; and the acorns in the grassy roads, and under the groups of oaks, showed all their colours, and especially the rosy hues where they had but just been covered by the cup. One by one I saw the things which made the autumn hedges so glorious and strange at a little distance: the yellow ash trees with some green leaves; the hoary and yellow willows; the hawthorns, purple and crimson and green; the briers, with most hips where there were fewest leaves; the green brambles with red fruit and black; tall, grey, and leafless thistles with a few small crimson flowers; the grey-green nettles with purple stems; the ragwort flowers; and on the long, green, wet grass the fallen leaves shining under red and yellow oaks; and through the olive lances of hazel the fields shining in patines of emerald. Doves cooed in the oaks, pheasants gleamed below. The air was full of the sweetness of the taste of blackberries, and the scent of mushrooms and of crumbling, wild carrot-seeds, and the colour of yellow, evening grass. The birches up on the hills above the road were golden, and like flowers. Between me and them a smouldering fire once or twice sent up dancing crimson flames, and the colour and perfume of the fire added themselves to the power of the calm, vast, and windless evening, of which the things I saw were as a few shells and anemones at the edge of a great sea. The valley waited and waited.

Edward Thomas, *The Heart of England*, 1906

He looked and smelt like Autumn's very brother, his face being sunburnt to wheat-colour, his eyes blue as corn-flowers, his sleeves and leggings dyed with fruit-stains, his hands clammy with the sweet juice of apples, his hat sprinkled with pips, and everywhere about him that atmosphere of cider which at its first return each season has such an indescribable fascination for those who have been born and bred among the orchards. Her heart rose from its late sadness like a released bough; her senses revelled in the sudden lapse back to Nature unadorned.

Thomas Hardy, *The Woodlanders*, 1887

Shortening Days at the Homestead

The first fire since the summer is lit, and is smoking into the room:
   The sun-rays thread it through, like woof-lines in a loom.
   Sparrows spurt from the hedge, whom misgivings appal
That winter did not leave last year for ever, after all.
     Like shock-headed urchins, spiny-haired,
     Stand pollard willows, their twigs just bared.

    Who is this coming with pondering pace,
    Black and ruddy, with white embossed,
    His eyes being black, and ruddy his face
    And the marge of his hair like morning frost?
      It's the cider-maker,
      And appletree-shaker,
    And behind him on wheels, in readiness,
    His mill, and tubs, and vat, and press.

Thomas Hardy

♣ September, blow soft, till the fruit's in the loft.

After Apple-Picking

    My long two-pointed ladder's sticking through a tree
    Toward heaven still,
    And there's a barrel that I didn't fill
    Beside it, and there may be two or three
    Apples I didn't pick upon some bough.
    But I am done with apple-picking now.
    Essence of winter sleep is on the night,
    The scent of apples: I am drowsing off.
    I cannot rub the strangeness from my sight
    I got from looking through a pane of glass
    I skimmed this morning from the drinking trough
    And held against the world of hoary grass.
    It melted, and I let it fall and break.

But I was well
Upon my way to sleep before it fell,
And I could tell
What form my dreaming was about to take.
Magnified apples appear and disappear,
Stem end and blossom end,
And every fleck of russet showing clear.
My instep arch not only keeps the ache,
It keeps the pressure of a ladder-round.
I feel the ladder sway as the boughs bend.
And I keep hearing from the cellar bin
The rumbling sound
Of load on load of apples coming in.
For I have had too much
Of apple-picking: I am overtired
Of the great harvest I myself desired.
There were ten thousand thousand fruit to touch,
Cherish in hand, lift down, and not let fall.
For all
That struck the earth,
No matter if not bruised or spiked with stubble,
Went sure to the cider-apple heap
As of no worth.
One can see what will trouble
This sleep of mine, whatever sleep it is.
Were he not gone,
The woodchuck could say whether it's like his
Long sleep, as I describe its coming on,
Or just some human sleep.

Robert Frost

To Meadows

Ye have been fresh and green,
    Ye have been fill'd with flowers;
And ye the walks have been
    Where maids have spent their hours.

You have beheld how they
    With wicker arks did come,
To kiss and bear away
    The richer cowslips home.

You've heard them sweetly sing,
    And seen them in a round;
Each virgin, like a spring,
    With honeysuckles crown'd.

But now, we see none here,
    Whose silvery feet did tread,
And with dishevell'd hair
    Adorn'd this smoother mead.

Like unthrifts, having spent
    Your stock, and needy grown,
You're left here to lament
    Your poor estates alone.

        Robert Herrick (1591–1674)

My wind is turned to bitter north,
    That was so soft a south before;
My sky, that shone so sunny bright,
    With foggy gloom is clouded o'er:
My gay green leaves are yellow-black,
    Upon the dank autumnal floor;
For love, departed once, comes back
    No more again, no more.

A roofless ruin lies my home,
    For winds to blow and rains to pour;
One frosty night befell, and lo!
    I find my summer days are o'er:
The heart bereaved, of why and how
    Unknowing, knows that yet before
It had what e'en to Memory now
    Returns no more, no more.

        A. H. Clough, from *Ambarvalia*, 1849

[Wednesday 30 September 1925]

. . . damp and close and over all the sense already of transmigration, of shedding one habit for another. My autumn coat is grown.

Virginia Woolf, Diary, Vol. 3 (1925–30), 1980

♣ Autumnal agues are long or mortal.

The two great planting months, October and November, are close upon us, and those gardeners who desire the maximum of reward with the minimum of labour would be well advised to concentrate upon the flowering shrubs and flowering trees. How deeply I regret that fifteen years ago, when I was forming my own garden, I did not plant these desirable objects in sufficient quantity. They would by now be large adults instead of the scrubby, spindly infants I contemplate with impatience as the seasons come round.

That error is one from which I would wish to save my fellow-gardeners, so, taking this opportunity, I implore them to secure trees and bushes from whatever nurseryman can supply them: they will give far less trouble than the orthodox herbaceous flowers, they will demand no annual division, many of them will require no pruning; in fact, all that many of them will ask of you is to watch them grow yearly into a greater splendour, and what more could be exacted of any plant?

V. Sackville-West's Garden Book, 1974

> I've brought you nuts and hops;
> And when the leaf drops, why, the walnut drops.
> Crack your first nut and light your first fire,
> Roast your first chestnut crisp on the bar;
> Make the logs sparkle, stir the blaze higher,
> Logs are as cheery as sun or as star,
> Logs we can find wherever we are.
> Spring one soft day will open the leaves,
> Spring one bright day will lure back the flowers;
> Never fancy my whistling wind grieves,
> Never fancy I've tears in my showers:
> Dance, night and days! and dance on, my hours!

Christina Rossetti (1830–94)

Nov. 8 [1874]—Walking with Wm. Splaine we saw a vast multitude of starlings making an unspeakable jangle. They would settle in a
row of trees; then, one tree after another, rising at a signal they looked
like a cloud of specks of black snuff or powder struck up from a brush
or broom or shaken from a wig; then they would sweep round in
whirlwinds—you could see the nearer and farther bow of the rings by
the size and blackness; many would be in one phase at once, all narrow
black flakes hurling round, then in another; then they would fall upon
a field and so on. Splaine wanted a gun: then 'there it would rain meat'
he said. I thought they must be full of enthusiasm and delight hearing
their cries and stirring and cheering one another

Gerard Manley Hopkins, Journal

The wood is becoming quite autumnal—there are effects of colour
which I very rarely find painted in Dutch pictures.

In the woods, yesterday toward evening, I was busy painting a
rather sloping ground covered with dry, mouldered beech leaves.
This ground was light and dark reddish-brown, made more so by the
shadows of trees casting more or less dark streaks over it, sometimes
half blotted out. The problem was—and I found it very difficult—to
get the depth of colour, the enormous force and solidity of that
ground—and while painting it I perceived for the very first time how
much light there still was in that dusk—to keep that light and at the
same time the glow and depth of that rich colour.

For you cannot imagine any carpet as splendid as that deep
brownish-red in the glow of an autumn evening sun, tempered by the
trees.

From that ground young beech trees spring up which catch the light
on one side and are brilliant green there; the shadowy sides of those
stems are a warm, deep black-green.

Behind those saplings, behind that brownish-red soil, is a sky very
delicate, bluish-grey, warm, hardly blue, all aglow—and against it all
is a hazy border of green and a network of little stems and yellowish
leaves. A few figures of wood gatherers are wandering around like
dark masses of mysterious shadows. The white cap of a woman
bending to reach a dry branch stands out suddenly against the deep
red-brown of the ground. A skirt catches the light—a shadow is
cast—a dark silhouette of a man appears above the underbrush. A

white bonnet, a cap, a shoulder, the bust of a woman moulds itself against the sky. Those figures are large and full of poetry—in the twilight of that deep shadowy tone they appear as enormous terra-cottas being modelled in a studio.

Van Gogh, *The Complete Letters of Vincent van Gogh*, 1958

The morns are meeker than they were—
The nuts are getting brown—
The berry's cheek is plumper—
The Rose is out of town.

The Maple wears a gayer scarf—
The field a scarlet gown—

Lest I should be old fashioned
I'll put a trinket on.

Emily Dickinson (1830–86)

October

The green elm with the one great bough of gold
Lets leaves into the grass slip, one by one.—
The short hill grass, the mushrooms small milk-white,
Harebell and scabious and tormentil,
That blackberry and gorse, in dew and sun,
Bow down to; and the wind travels too light
To shake the fallen birch leaves from the fern;
The gossamers wander at their own will.
At heavier steps than birds' the squirrels scold.

The late year has grown fresh again and new
As Spring, and to the touch is not more cool
Than it is warm to the gaze; and now I might
As happy be as earth is beautiful,
Were I some other or with earth could turn
In alternation of violet and rose,

Harebell and snowdrop, at their season due,
And gorse that has no time not to be gay.
But if this be not happiness, who knows?
Some day I shall think this a happy day,
And this mood by the name of melancholy
Shall no more blackened and obscured be.

Edward Thomas, 1915

Equinox

Heads down now the hard weather's come, the kids
snap out of school. At four the greengrocer
stacks his pavement spread, trolleys it inside.

No sunset. The sky at chromatic north.
No cloud, only this north wind of colour,
the sun's recessional, the equinox,
when fire and brimstone behave like angels.

Low, impermanent as a shanty-town
lie the bare precincts, the dormitory streets
to these trebles of gold, this green alto.

Over the playing fields, at the street's end,
the cold declensions of October light.

Roger Garfitt, *West of Elm*, 1975

How well I know what I mean to do
　　When the long dark Autumn evenings come,
And where, my soul, is thy pleasant hue?
　　With the music of all thy voices, dumb
In life's November too!

I shall be found by the fire, suppose,
　　O'er a great wise book as beseemeth age,
While the shutters flap as the cross-wind blows,
　　And I turn the page, and I turn the page,
Not verse now, only prose!

Robert Browning, from 'By the Fire-side', 1855

The 31st of October is called Hallowe'en. It is the night when, according to folklore, witches, devils, fairies, hobgoblins and all the imps of earth and air hold their annual holiday. Years ago, people lit fires to keep these creatures away, but nowadays if we have fires it is for roasting chestnuts. However, we still dress up and have Hallowe'en parties; and people play the old game of ducking for apples floating in a bowl of water. These have to be caught between the player's teeth. The size of the apple you catch is supposed to show the size of your future fortune.

Septima, *Something to Do*, 1966

Nutting

The sun had stooped his westward clouds to win
Like weary traveller seeking for an Inn
When from the hazelly wood we glad descried
The ivied gateway by the pasture side
Long had we sought for nutts amid the shade
Where silence fled the rustle that we made
When torn by briars and brushed by sedges rank
We left the wood and on the velvet bank
Of short sward pasture ground we sat us down
To shell our nutts before we reached the town
The near hand stubble field with mellow glower
Showed the dimmed blaze of poppys still in flower
And sweet the molehills smelt we sat upon
And now the thymes in bloom but where is pleasure gone

Nutters

The rural occupations of the year
Are each a fitting theme for pastoral song
And pleasing in our autumn paths appear
The groups of nutters as they chat along
The woodland rides in strangest dissabille
Maids jacketed grotesque in garments ill
Hiding their elegance of shape—her ways

Her voice of music makes her woman still
Aught else the error of a carless gaze
Might fancy uncouth rustics noising bye
With laugh and chat and scraps of morning news
Till met the hazel shades and in they hie
Garbed suiting to the toil—the morning dews
Among the underwood are hardly dry

John Clare (1793–1864)

Wild Peaches

I

When the world turns completely upside down
You say we'll emigrate to the Eastern Shore
Aboard a river-boat from Baltimore;
We'll live among wild peach trees, miles from town,
You'll wear a coonskin cap, and I a gown
Homespun, dyed butternut's dark gold colour.
Lost, like your lotus-eating ancestor,
We'll swim in milk and honey till we drown.

The winter will be short, the summer long,
The autumn amber-hued, sunny and hot,
Tasting of cider and of scuppernong;
All seasons sweet, but autumn best of all.
The squirrels in their silver fur will fall
Like falling leaves, like fruit, before your shot.

2

The autumn frosts will lie upon the grass
Like bloom on grapes of purple-brown and gold.
The misted early mornings will be cold;
The little puddles will be roofed with glass.
The sun, which burns from copper into brass,
Melts these at noon, and makes the boys unfold
Their knitted mufflers; full as they can hold,
Fat pockets dribble chestnuts as they pass.

Peaches grow wild, and pigs can live in clover;
A barrel of salted herrings lasts a year;
The spring begins before the winter's over.
By February you may find the skins
Of garter snakes and water moccasins
Dwindled and harsh, dead-white and cloudy-clear.

3

When April pours the colours of a shell
Upon the hills, when every little creek
Is shot with silver from the Chesapeake
In shoals new-minted by the ocean swell,
When strawberries go begging, and the sleek
Blue plums lie open to the blackbird's beak,
We shall live well—we shall live very well.

The months between the cherries and the peaches
Are brimming cornucopias which spill
Fruits red and purple, sombre-bloomed and black;
Then, down rich fields and frosty river beaches
We'll trample bright persimmons, while you kill
Bronze partridge, speckled quail, and canvasback.

4

Down to the Puritan marrow of my bones
There's something in this richness that I hate.
I love the look, austere, immaculate,
Of landscapes drawn in pearly monotones.

There's something in my very blood that owns
Bare hills, cold silver on a sky of slate,
A thread of water, churned to milky spate
Streaming through slanted pastures fenced with
    stones.

I love those skies, thin blue or snowy gray,
Those fields sparse-planted, rendering meagre sheaves;
That spring, briefer than apple-blossom's breath,
Summer, so much too beautiful to stay,
Swift autumn, like a bonfire of leaves,
And sleepy winter, like the sleep of death.

Elinor Wylie, *Nets to Catch the Wind*, 1911

The sight of the bent trees along the Lincolnshire marshland and the landmark of Winterton Church tower north of Yarmouth brings to mind the stories of the Cromer lifeboat, and for how long the north-easter was justly dreaded by the Newcastle colliers on the way to and from London if it caught them on the long stretch between Winterton Ness and Flamborough Head. Defoe mentions how in one year (1692) two hundred ships were wrecked in a single storm.

Gordon Manley, *Climate and the British Scene*, 1952

♣ November take flail, let ships no more sail.

It was a rimy morning, and very damp. I had seen the damp lying on the outside of my little window, as if some goblin had been crying there all night, and using the window for a pocket-handkerchief. Now, I saw the damp lying on the bare hedges and spare grass, like a coarser sort of spiders' webs; hanging itself from twig to twig and blade to blade. On every rail and gate, wet lay clammy; and the marsh-mist was so thick, that the wooden finger on the post directing people to our village—a direction which they never accepted, for they never came there—was invisible to me until I was quite close under it. Then, as I looked up at it, while it dripped, it seemed to my oppressed conscience like a phantom devoting me to the Hulks.

The mist was heavier yet when I got out upon the marshes, so that instead of my running at everything, everything seemed to run at me. This was very disagreeable to a guilty mind. The gates and dykes and banks came bursting at me through the mist, as if they cried as plainly as could be, 'A boy with Somebody-else's pork pie! Stop him!' The cattle came upon me with like suddenness, staring out of their eyes, and steaming out of their nostrils, 'Holloa, young thief!' One black ox, with a white cravat on—who even had to my awakened conscience something of a clerical air—fixed me so obstinately with his eyes, and moved his blunt head round in such an accusatory manner as I moved round, that I blubbered out to him, 'I couldn't help it, sir! It wasn't for myself I took it!' Upon which he put down his head, blew a cloud of smoke out of his nose, and vanished with a kick-up of his hind-legs and a flourish of his tail.

Charles Dickens, *Great Expectations*, 1860–1

Dear Sir,

While I was in Sussex last autumn my residence was at the village near Lewes, from whence I had formerly the pleasure of writing to you. On the first of November I remarked that the old tortoise, formerly mentioned, began first to dig the ground in order to the forming its hybernaculum, which it had fixed on just beside a great tuft of hepaticas. It scrapes out the ground with its fore-feet, and throws it up over its back with its hind; but the motion of its legs is ridiculously slow, little exceeding the hour-hand of a clock; and suitable to the composure of an animal said to be a whole month in performing one feat of copulation. Nothing can be more assiduous than this creature night and day in scooping the earth, and forcing its great body into the cavity; but, as the noons of that season proved unusually warm and sunny, it was continually interrupted, and called forth by the heat in the middle of the day; and though I continued there till the thirteenth of November, yet the work remained un-finished. Harsher weather, and frosty mornings, would have quick-ened its operations. No part of its behaviour ever struck me more than the extreme timidity it always expresses with regard to rain; for though it has a shell that would secure it against the wheel of a loaded cart, yet does it discover as much solicitude about rain as a lady dressed in all her best attire, shuffling away on the first sprinklings, and running its head up in a corner. If attended to, it becomes an excellent weather-glass; for as sure as it walks elate, and as it were on tiptoe, feeding with great earnestness in a morning, so sure will it rain before night. It is totally a diurnal animal, and never pretends to stir after it becomes dark. The tortoise, like other reptiles, has an arbitrary stomach as well as lungs; and can refrain from eating as well as breathing for a great part of the year. When first awakened it eats nothing; nor again in the autumn before it retires: through the height of the summer it feeds voraciously, devouring all the food that comes in its way. I was much taken in with its sagacity in discerning those that do it kind offices; for, as soon as the good old lady comes in sight who has waited on it for more than thirty years, it hobbles towards its benefactress with awkward alacrity; but remains inattentive to strangers. Thus not only 'the ox knoweth his owner, and the ass his master's crib,' but the most abject reptile and torpid of beings distinguishes the hand that feeds it, and is touched with the feelings of gratitude!

I am, etc., etc.

P.S. In about three days after I left Sussex the tortoise retired into the ground under the hepatica.

Gilbert White, *The Natural History of Selborne*, 1789

FRIDAY 12TH NOVEMBER

Another heavy dew and mists this morning, but in spite of the sun it is still muddy under foot. There is not enough strength in the autumn sun to dry the land before the next morning's dew.

The stock looks well everywhere, and there is little doubt now that the yearlings' ringworm is disappearing, like Emily's. One cure seems to be as effective as the other.

Graham boiled up the milking equipment this morning. Hygiene in the milking parlour is vital, and we always wash through the milking equipment twice a day after milking, and then scrub down the parlour. Then once a week we give the whole machine a thorough clean through, and remove all the rubber and metal parts to boil them for sterilisation. During these next 6 to 8 weeks in the temporary parlour it is going to be very important to be thorough.

SATURDAY 13TH

The mists have turned to frost, and all the water pipes to the outdoor parlour were frozen up this morning, so that Graham couldn't even begin milking until 9 o'clock when they had thawed out. The milk lorry comes to the four crossways at 10.45, so time was short. He just made it, arriving at the milkstand with the churns at the same time as the lorry.

When we were feeding hay to the herd after milking, we took away the last bales in the first bay of the Dutch barn. It has disappeared fast and spring is still a long way off. John wakes up at night sometimes and worries whether we shall have enough. At night he never thinks so, but by the morning things seem more promising.

Michael Morpurgo, All Around the Year, 1979

The Plough-driver's art consisteth herein, that he drive the yoked oxen evenly, neither smiting nor pricking nor grieving them. Such should not be melancholy or wrathful, but cheerful, jocund and full of song, that by their melody and song the oxen may in a manner rejoice in their labour. Such a ploughman should bring the fodder with his own hands, and love his oxen and sleep with them by night, tickling and combing and rubbing them with straw; keeping them well in all respects, and guarding their forage or provender from theft. . . . If he finds other beasts in their pasture, he must impound them. He and the hinds, when plough-time is over, must dike and delve, thresh, fence, clean the water-courses and do other such-like profitable works.

From 'Fleta', a thirteenth-century treatise on Rural Economy,
edited by John Selden in 1647

To Autumn

Season of mists and mellow fruitfulness,
   Close bosom-friend of the maturing sun;
Conspiring with him how to load and bless
   With fruit the vines that round the thatch-eves run;
To bend with apples the moss'd cottage-trees,
   And fill all fruit with ripeness to the core;
     To swell the gourd, and plump the hazel shells
   With a sweet kernel; to set budding more,

And still more, later flowers for the bees,
Until they think warm days will never cease,
    For Summer has o'er-brimmed their clammy cells.

Who hath not seen thee oft amid thy store?
    Sometimes whoever seeks abroad may find
Thee sitting careless on a granary floor,
    Thy hair soft-lifted by the winnowing wind;
Or on a half-reap'd furrow sound asleep,
    Drows'd with the fume of poppies, while thy hook
      Spares the next swath and all its twined flowers:
And sometimes like a gleaner thou dost keep
    Steady thy laden head across a brook;
    Or by a cyder-press, with patient look,
      Thou watchest the last oozings hours by hours.

Where are the song of Spring? Ay, where are they?
    Think not of them, thou hast thy music too,—
While barred clouds bloom the soft-dying day,
    And touch the stubble-plains with rosy hue;
Then in a wailful choir the small gnats mourn
    Among the river sallows, borne aloft
      Or sinking as the light wind lives or dies;
And full-grown lambs loud bleat from hilly bourn;
    Hedge-crickets sing; and now with treble soft
    The red-breast whistles from a garden-croft;
      And gathering swallows twitter in the skies.

                         John Keats, 1820

Upon the Dark Thick Mist Happening on the 27 of November 1674

Though it be not strange to see frequent mists, clouds and rains in England, as many ancient describers of this country have noted, yet I could not [but] take notice of a very great mist which happened upon the 27 of the last November, and from thence have taken this occasion to propose something of mists, clouds and rains unto your candid considerations.

Herein mists may well deserve the first place as being if not the first in nature, yet the first meteor mentioned in Scripture, and soon after the creation, for it is said Genesis 2. that God had not yet caused to rain upon the earth, but a mist went up from the earth and watered the whole face of the ground, for it might take a longer time for the elevation of vapours sufficient to make a congregation of clouds able to afford any store of showers and rain in so early days of the world.

Thick vapours not ascending high but hanging about the earth and covering the surface of it are commonly called mists; if they ascend high they are termed clouds. They remain upon the earth, till they either fall down or are attenuated, rarified and scattered.

This great mist was not only observable about London but in remote parts of England and as we hear in Holland, so that it was of larger extent then mists are commonly apprehended to be, most men conceiving that they reach not much beyond the places where they behold them. Mist[s] make an obscure air but they beget not darkness, for the atoms and particules thereof admit the light, but if the matter thereof be very thick, close, and condensed, the mist grows considerably obscure and like a cloud, so the miraculous and palpable darkness of Ægypt is conceived to have been effected by an extraordinary dark mist or a kind of cloud spread over the land of Ægypt, and also miraculously restrained from the neighbour land of Goshen.

Mists and fogs containing commonly vegetable spirits, when they dissolve and return upon the earth, may fecundate and add some fertility unto it, but they may be more unwholesome in great cities then in country habitations, for they consist of vapours not only elevated from simple watery and humid places, but also the exhalations of draughts, common shores, and fetid places and decoctions used by unwholesome and sordid manufactures; and also hindering the seacoal smoke from ascending and passing away, it is conjoined with the mist and drawn in by the breath, all which may produce bad effects, inquinate the blood, and produce catarrhs and coughs. Sereins, well known in hot countries, cause headache, toothache, and swelled faces, but they seem to have their original from subtle invisible nitrous and piercing exhalations caused by a strong heat of the sun, which falling after sunset produce the effects mentioned.

Sir Thomas Browne

Song

Fall, leaves, fall; die, flowers, away;
Lengthen night and shorten day;
Every leaf speaks bliss to me
Fluttering from the autumn tree.
I shall smile when wreaths of snow
Blossom where the rose should grow;
I shall sing when night's decay
Ushers in a drearier day.

Emily Brontë (1818–48)

For several days now this white fog has occluded the rest of the world. Occasionally the sun shows a pale silver disc overhead, giving illusion of warmth; then the drifting cold mist swirls silently over the hedge, and I must either continue to dig or put on my coat again.

The mist moves like the spirit of silence not yet dead. Rooks and jackdaws flying over the field suddenly appear, to veer as suddenly, and vanish again. A robin, bird always to appear when man is digging, flits between worm-picking pauses from one clod to another.

The temperature appears to vary much from hour to hour. Two hours ago it was surely freezing, the dead tufts of grass in the uncropped field were crisp to walk through; now the hoar is gone as it mysteriously settled.

Three hours ago, at eleven o'clock, the white owl sailed from its beech tree in Windwhistle Spinney and flew high east, presumably to its hunting. At noon it came back, with the same determined flight, fifty feet high, and settled in its usual fork. Had it gone down to the forsaken iron mines of the valley, disturbed in its day-dozing by thoughts of a mate?

Last fall a dying barn-owl was found in a rabbit gin two fields away, and this may have been its old mate. Owls appear to pair for life.

A grey squirrel has found my small plantation, for many of the tops of the various pines are gnawn off and lie scattered underneath the trees. If it be a grey American squirrel, then it is the first I have heard of in this district of North Devon.

A sleepy queen-wasp stung me this morning as I was frying my breakfast bacon. Apparently she chose the handle of my frying-pan for a place of hibernation, beside a small, terrified spider, and the warmth of the fire awoke her to action and defence.

Half an hour later, routing in my tool-shed for a sharp-pointed shovel called a backbreaker by the District Council road workers who never exert themselves unduly, I was stung by another queen wasp. Now it may be coincidence, but soon afterwards the pains in my back, due to rheumatism, ceased; and thereafter I felt more in harmony with the world.

Henry Williamson, 'The Harmony of Nature', *Collected Nature Stories*, 1970

At Day-Close in November

The ten hours' light is abating,
    And a late bird wings across,
Where the pines, like waltzers waiting,
    Give their black heads a toss.

Beech leaves, that yellow the noon-time,
    Float past like specks in the eye;
I set every tree in my June time,
    And now they obscure the sky.

And the children who ramble through here
    Conceive that there never has been
A time when no tall trees grew here,
    That none will in time be seen.

Thomas Hardy, 1914

In a gently heaving land, which was broken every three or four miles by a sudden, castled crag, Autumn was perfect, but with just a touch of sublimity added to its beauty by the thought that, on the next day or the next, winter would fall upon her unsuspected, as Pizarro and the Spanish cavalry fell upon that noble Indian, Atahualpa, who had come up to them in peace and meekness and pomp, upon a golden litter, among thousands of his gentle subjects, making music and decorated with gold, and expecting to meet the gods.

The bells of the cattle on broad, yellow lawns were ringing. Squirrels glowed in the road; the heavy rooks let fall the acorns among the leaves continually. The last beams of the sun reached now a circle of high bracken on a far-off hill, and reached it alone and transfigured it with strong quiet light; and then made one brown hill seem to be consumed in a golden glow, while the next hill was sombre; and again devoted themselves to a group of beeches that shone ruddy, branch and leaf and bole, and divine and majestic and unrelated to the cattle passing underneath.

The sun went down; wild-duck and moorhen cried and scudded on the calm, winding, silver river at my feet; and in a field beyond, that retained so much liquid and lugubrious light as to seem a green water, some laughing boys in white and yellow played football, without regarding the silver and purple, frosty sky, to which, nevertheless, their shrill voices added something, from which their movements took something, that was glorious and pathetic. And near by, dark oxen with rocking gait thrust their horns up into the sky as they approached the bridge.

Edward Thomas, *The Heart of England*, 1906

Summer for England ends: simple and likeable
This moving a clock's hands, as if saying
'With this act we cancel formally the summer;
We'll have no lingering last-rose last-post sweetness
Of breath-moist bugle flowering in the dusk.
Winterwards turn we the face of time.'

James Reeves, from 'The Hour and the Storm', 1938

WINTER

Our word, winter, shares its roots with 'wet' and 'water': what, then, can we say for it? The positive answer is presumably to be found, at least by the young, in the exhilarations offered by snow and ice; and the more judicious of us may succeed in ameliorating its drearer severities by turning to the social amenities of enforced companionableness. It is hardly surprising that Dr Johnson perceived winter as the time when we come together for conversation, for social warmth at the hearth.

Yet, making all due allowance, many of us find it an almost intolerably sombre season: the fogs of November, followed by the winter solstice and its shortest day, and then the severities of January freezings and February icings. Certainly grey clouds are too much with us, too often and for too long. We begin to suspect that the sun is, indeed, faltering or failing.

Hence, presumably, the often desperate remedies—the festivals, the parties, the strenuous cheerfulness of Christmas crackers, the feeble candle-light, and self-indulgence at the table. Strange that, after all, we do not actually hibernate.

The Coming of Winter

I have news for you; the stag bells, winter snows, summer has gone.

Wind high and cold, the sun low, short its course, the sea running high.

Deep red the bracken, its shape is lost; the wild goose has raised its accustomed cry.

Cold has seized the birds' wings; season of ice, this is my news.

Anon., 9th century

Picture Books in Winter

Summer fading, winter comes—
Frosty mornings, tingling thumbs,
Window robins, winter rooks,
And the picture story-books.

Water now is turned to stone
Nurse and I can walk upon;
Still we find the flowing brooks
In the picture story-books.

All the pretty things put by,
Wait upon the children's eye,
Sheep and shepherds, trees and crooks,
In the picture story-books.

We may see how all things are,
Seas and cities, near and far,
And the flying fairies' looks,
In the picture story-books.

How am I to sing your praise,
Happy chimney-corner days,
Sitting safe in nursery nooks,
Reading picture story-books?

Robert Louis Stevenson (1850–94)

Over a large part of the British Isles the more impressive extremes of our winter weather occur with somewhat dangerous rarity. Further, their effects on our consciousness tend to be mitigated in towns and cities. To this we must add the fact that a rapid improvement in the amenities and ease of transport and in the efficient heating of public buildings has taken place during four decades, 1898–1939, characterized by a predominance of mild winters.

Eighty per cent of our people live in towns; hence many of our people are inclined to forget that snow is still a very important factor in our northern uplands, perhaps more so on account of the very wide variations in its occurrence, whether in amount, persistence, or season of year. Snow came back noticeably into the Londoner's consciousness, for the first time for several years, in December 1938. Since then the severe winters of 1940–41–42, the cold January of 1945, the very severe February of 1947 and the cold December of 1950 have affected all Britain. February 1954 and 1955 were snowy; February 1956 severely cold.

Gordon Manley, *Climate and the British Scene*, 1952

♣ Winter finds out what summer lays up.

> Blow, blow, thou winter wind,
> Thou are not so unkind
>   As man's ingratitude;
> Thy tooth is not so keen,
> Because thou art not seen,
>   Although thy breath be rude.
> Heigh-ho! sing, heigh-ho! unto the green holly:
> Most friendship is feigning, most loving mere folly.
>   Then heigh-ho! the holly!
>   This life is most jolly.
>
> Freeze, freeze, thou bitter sky,
> That dost not bite so nigh
>   As benefits forgot:
> Though thou the waters warp,
> Thy sting is not so sharp

As friend remember'd not.
Heigh-ho! sing, heigh-ho! unto the green holly:
Most friendship is feigning, most loving mere folly.
Then heigh-ho! the holly!
This life is most jolly.

William Shakespeare, *As You Like It*, *c*.1598

To Winter

'O Winter! bar thine adamantine doors:
The north is thine; there hast thou built thy dark
Deep-founded habitation. Shake not thy roofs,
Nor bend thy pillars with thine iron car.'

He hears me not, but o'er the yawning deep
Rides heavy; his storms are unchain'd, sheathèd
In ribbèd steel; I dare not lift mine eyes,
For he hath rear'd his sceptre o'er the world.

Lo! now the direful monster, whose skin clings
To his strong bones, strides o'er the groaning rocks:
He withers all in silence, and in his hand
Unclothes the earth, and freezes up frail life.

He takes his seat upon the cliffs—the mariner
Cries in vain. Poor little wretch, that deal'st
With storms!—till heaven smiles, and the monster
Is driv'n yelling to his caves beneath mount Hecla.

William Blake, 1783

[Davos, 29 November 1877]

We have been sledge driving today—only to Kulm & back—but it has been such an ethereal magical unimaginable expedition—an aeon of enchantment condensed into one afternoon hour—that I must write to you about it. If you & Maggie are really thinking of coming, as I trust you are, it is right you should know what lovely things are in store for you.

The strong level sunlight falls upon the snow; & where the light is, the snow-surface sparkles with a myriad stars, snow-flowers & crystals shaped like fern-leaf-moss. Where there is no light, the shadow is no less blue than the sky; so that the whole journey is like sailing through tracts of light-irradiate heavens & interstellar spaces of the clearest & most flawless ether. The movement is more gliding than any thing I can describe. The air as one drinks it, is like the air of highest glaciers. As we go, the bells keep up a drowsy tinkling at the horse's head. Then the whole landscape is transfigured—lifted high up out of its commonplaceness. The little hills are Monte Rosas & Mont Blancs. Scale is quite annihilated; & nothing tell but form. Such sweeps of pure untroubled snows—fold over fold of undulating softness! And the pines, some hung with icicles, some bowed with snow, glow golden-green & red & brown—each tiniest trace of colour telling. The chalets are more like fancy houses than ever: waist-deep in stores of winter wood: wonderful in their tints of madder & bistre: with fantastic icicles hanging from the eaves & great folds of snow like coverlids curving from the roof in towards the windows. The lake is not frozen; & its reflections are as perfect as ever.

Words cannot convey the sense of immaterial, aerial, lucid beauty —the feeling of purity & aloofness from all sordid things—the magic of the light & movement. It is more musical—more like a spirit mood of Shelley's lyric-singing than anything else. The only thing comparable to it is rowing on the waters round Amalfio. And this is somehow more remote from earthliness.

John Addington Symonds (1840–93), Letters

Signs of Winter

Tis winter plain the images around
Protentious tell us of the closing year
Short grows the stupid day the moping fowl
Go roost at noon—upon the mossy barn
The thatcher hangs and lays the frequent yaum
Nudged close to stop the rain that drizzling falls
With scarce one interval of sunny sky
For weeks still leeking on that sulky gloom
Muggy and close a doubt twixt night and day
The sparrow rarely chirps the thresher pale
Twanks with sharp measured raps the weary frail

Thump after thump right tiresome to the ear
The hedger lonesome brustles at his toil
And shepherds trudge the fields without a song

The cat runs races with her tail—the dog
Leaps oer the orchard hedge and knarls the grass
The swine run round and grunt and play with straw
Snatching out hasty mouthfuls from the stack
Sudden upon the elm tree tops the crows
Unceremonious visit pays and croaks
Then swops away—from mossy barn the owl
Bobs hasty out—wheels round and scared as soon
As hastily retires—the ducks grow wild
And from the muddy pond fly up and wheel
A circle round the village and soon tired
Plunge in the pond again—the maids in haste
Snatch from the orchard hedge the mizled cloaths
And laughing hurry in to keep them dry

John Clare (1793–1864)

The morning had been lovely, but during our singing practice after
evening Church at about half past four began the Great Storm of 1872.
Suddenly the wind rose up and began to roar at the Tower window and
shake the panes and lash the glass with torrents of rain. It grew very
dark. The storm increased and we struggled home in torrents of rain
and tempests of wind so fearful that we could hardly force our way
across the Common to the Rectory. All the evening the roaring S.W.
wind raged more and more furious. It seemed as if the windows on the
west side of the house must be blown in. The glass cracked and
strained and bent and the storm shrieked and wailed and howled like
multitudes of lost spirits. I went out to see where the cows were,
fearing that the large elms in the Avenue might fall and crush them.
The trees were writhing, swaying, rocking, lashing their arms wildly
and straining terribly in the tempest but I could not see that any were
gone yet. The twin firs in the orchard seemed the worst off, they gave
the wind such a power and purchase, with their heavy green boughs,
and their tops were swaying fearfully and bending nearly double
under the tremendous strain.

The moon was high and the clouds drove wild and fast across her face. Dark storms and thick black drifts were hurrying up out of the west, where the Almighty was making the clouds His chariot and walking upon the wings of the wind. Now and then the moon looked out for a moment wild and terrified through a savage rent in the storm.

The cows were safe in the cowyard and the door shut, though how I cannot tell. They must have gone there for shelter and it seemed as if the Lord had shut them in. As I stood at the cowyard gate leading into the field I was almost frightened at the fury of the wind, the blasts were so awful that I feared one of the great elms must fall. Sometimes the tempest rose to such a furious and ungovernable pitch as if hell had been let loose, that it seemed as if something must go, and as if the very world itself must give way and be shattered to atoms. The very beasts seemed frightened and the dog lay close in his kennel and would not come out. I went round to the front of the house and stood on the stone steps and wondered at the wind and thought of the poor people on Clyro Hill and prayed for those at sea. 'For at his word the stormy wind ariseth which lifteth up the waves thereof.' The whole world seemed to be groaning and straining under the press of that dreadful wind.

All the evening the wind roared and thundered and the tempest grew wilder and more wild, and if damage was done we could not hear it. Everything was drowned in the roar and thunder of the storm. The wind howled down the chimney, the room was full of smoke and every now and then the fire flaught out into the room in tongues of flame beaten down with a smother of sparks and smoke.

All night the tempest raged and when daylight broke there was a scene of ruin and devastation. The Acacia was safe, but a Scotch fir in the avenue near the white gate had been torn up by the roots and in falling had carried away the limb of a beech, the Banksia rose and the yellow Cape jessamine had been torn in a vast mat from the South wall and were lying prostrate on the terrace leaving a great space of the house white and bare and studded with nails. The great leaning elm at the bottom corner of the field south west of the Rectory had gone in the night, happily killing no cattle. It had been torn up by the roots and had carried away with it bank and rails and all leaving a huge gulf where the bank had been. The top of the tree was beaten all to pieces, and beyond two young ashes of ours in the next hedge had been blown down. No one heard the crash of the falling trees. It was impossible to tell when they went. The raging of the awful tempest drowned everything.

When I went to the school I was relieved to see the old Stocks Tree standing uninjured, while many younger trees had been torn up or broken off. An elm in the meadow behind the school had been broken short off, half of it broken off and the rest still standing. Accounts came pouring in by the school children and others of damage done in different parts of the parish.

An elm fell at Cocklebury and crushed a cow to death. The Awdrys at Monkton were sitting round the drawing room fire last night when the chimney stack fell, the bricks, stones and mortar came thundering down the chimney and drove the fire and soot and dust and ashes all over the room, damaging the furniture and carpet considerably.

Ninety trees fell in Savernake Park and Forest. The Pinnacles of St. Thomas's Church in Exeter blown down upon the roof of the Church during evening service. Two lives lost in Bristol by the falling of a house.

At Weymouth and Portland the people said that the late heavy gale which drove the *Royal Adelaide* ashore and wrecked her in the Chesil was only a gentle summer breeze compared with the dreadful storm that blew last night. But on the whole the damage is not so great as I should have expected. No ships came ashore on the fatal Chesil Bank.

Revd Francis Kilvert, *Diary*, 8–9 December 1872

Frost

What swords and spears, what daggers bright
He arms the morning with! How light
His powder is, that's fit to lie
On the wings of a butterfly!
What milk-white clothing he has made
For every little twig and blade!
What curious silver work is shown
On wood and iron, glass and stone!
'If you, my slim Jack Frost, can trace
This work so fine, so full of grace,
Tell me,' I said, 'before I go—
Where is your plump young sister, Snow?'

W. H. Davies (1871–1940)

Snow

In the gloom of whiteness,
In the great silence of snow,
A child was sighing
And bitterly saying: 'Oh,
They have killed a white bird up there on her nest,
The down is fluttering from her breast.'
And still it fell through that dusky brightness
On the child crying for the bird of the snow.

Edward Thomas, 1915

   And in the frosty season, when the sun
Was set, and visible for many a mile
The cottage windows blazed through twilight gloom,
I heeded not their summons: happy time
It was indeed for all of us—for me
It was a time of rapture! Clear and loud
The village clock tolled six,—I wheeled about,
Proud and exulting like an untired horse
That cares not for his home. All shod with steel,
We hissed along the polished ice in games
Confederate, imitative of the chase
And woodland pleasures,—the resounding horn,
The pack loud chiming, and the hunted hare.
So through the darkness and the cold we flew,
And not a voice was idle; with the din
Smitten, the precipices rang aloud;
The leafless trees and every icy crag
Tinkled like iron; while far distant hills
Into the tumult sent an alien sound
Of melancholy not unnoticed, while the stars
Eastward were sparkling clear, and in the west
The orange sky of evening died away.
Not seldom from the uproar I retired
Into a silent bay, or sportively
Glanced sideway, leaving the tumultuous throng,
To cut across the reflex of a star

That fled, and, flying still before me, gleamed
Upon the glassy plain; and oftentimes,
When we had given our bodies to the wind,
And all the shadowy banks on either side
Came sweeping through the darkness, spinning still
The rapid line of motion, then at once
Have I, reclining back upon my heels,
Stopped short; yet still the solitary cliffs
Wheeled by me—even as if the earth had rolled
With visible motion her diurnal round!
Behind me did they stretch in solemn train,
Feebler and feebler, and I stood and watched
Till all was tranquil as a dreamless sleep.

William Wordsworth, from *The Prelude*, Book I, 1805

There had been just snow enough to cover the earth and all its covers with one sheet of pure and uniform white, and just time enough since the snow had fallen to allow the hedges to be freed of their fleecy load, and clothed with a delicate coating of rime. The atmosphere was deliciously calm; soft, even mild, in spite of the thermometer; no perceptible air, but a stillness that might almost be felt, the sky, rather gray than blue, throwing out in bold relief the snow-covered roofs of our village, and the rimy trees that rise above them, and the sun shining dimly as through a veil, giving a pale fair light, like the moon, only brighter. There was a silence, too, that might become the moon, as we stood at our little gate looking up the quiet street; a Sabbath-like pause of work and play, rare on a work-day; nothing was audible but the pleasant hum of frost, that low monotonous sound, which is perhaps the nearest approach that life and nature can make to absolute silence. The very waggons as they come down the hill along the beaten track of crisp yellowish frost-dust, glide along like shadows; even May's bounding footsteps, at her height of glee and of speed, fall like snow upon snow.

Mary Russell Mitford, *Our Village*, 1824–32

Snow, next to flowers and sunshine and perhaps the rainbow, is the loveliest of all natural events, certainly the loveliest of all winter happenings, lovelier than frost or winter moonlight. And in England

it comes seldom enough to be a rare joy and never lingers long enough to be wearisome. It falls and performs its brief white miracle of transformation and vanishes again before the senses have grown used to that amazing whiteness, the beauty of blue bays of sky opening above the snow-lined trees, and the strange stillness of the silent land.

I am not talking now of the snow which falls in towns, and which is not at all the most lovely winter phenomenon, but probably the most depressing and most hated: only of snow which falls in the country, opening out in a wonderful way its distances, creating a feeling of great light and tranquil spaciousness in its open fields and a strange softness and silence in its woods, the trees never moving under the weight of

snow, the bird-life suspended except for the dainty pattering of pheasants among bracken and bramble and over snow-sprinkled chestnut leaves and the wild cry of a mad blackbird escaping through the hazels. There is no stillness in the world like the stillness of the world under snow. The stillness of summer is made up in effect of sounds, of many little drowsy sounds like the warm monotonous moan of pigeons, the changeless tune of invisible yellowhammers, the dreamy fluttering of thick leaves, sounds which together send the air half to sleep and create that singing silence which is almost a tangible thing in the heart of warm summer afternoons.

But the silence of snow is absolute; the silence of death and suspense. It is as though the snow has a paralysing effect, deadening the wind, freezing the voices of the birds. It is a silence which is absolutely complete in itself; not an illusion like the summer silence, not made up of sounds somnolently repeated. It is pure tranquillity and soundlessness, profoundest and most wonderful when the snow has finally ceased; full of expectancy and broken by the occasional uneasy cries of rooks when snow has still to come. And the fall of snow on snow, through the silence of snow, is the perfection of beauty: a lovely paradox of silence and movement, of stillness and life, the twinkling and fluttering and dancing of the new snow against the old.

H. E. Bates, *Through the Woods*, 1969

Snow is a general informer, betraying the footsteps of every creature, great and small. The poacher and the gamekeeper are equally on the alert, while it lies freshly upon the ground; the one to track game, the other vermin; and thousands of polecats, weasels, stoats, rats, otters, badgers, and similar little nightly depredators, are traced to their hiding-places in old buildings, banks, and hollow trees, and marked for certain destruction. The poacher, particularly on moonlight nights, makes havoc with game. Partridges, nestled down in a heap on the stubble, are conspicuous objects; and hares, driven for food to gardens and turnip-fields, are destroyed by hundreds. Wood-pigeons are killed in great numbers on cabbage and turnip-fields by day, and by moonlight are shot in the trees where they roost. Larks frequent stubbles in vast flocks, and are destroyed by gun or net.

William Howitt, *Book of the Seasons*, 1833

Footprints in the snow have been unfailing provokers of sentiment ever since snow was first a white wonder in this drab-coloured world of ours. In a poetry-book presented to one of us by an aunt, there was a poem by one Wordsworth, in which they stood out strongly—with a picture all to themselves, too—but we didn't think very highly either of the poem or the sentiment. Footprints in the snow, now, were quite another matter, and we grasped Crusoe's attitude of mind much more easily than Wordsworth's. Excitement and mystery, curiosity and suspense—these were the only sentiments that tracks, whether in sand or in snow, were able to arouse in us.

We had awakened early that winter morning, puzzled at first by the added light that filled the room. Then, when the truth at last fully dawned on us and we knew that snow-balling was no longer a wistful dream, but a solid certainty waiting for us outside, it was a mere brute fight for the necessary clothes, and the lacing of boots seemed a clumsy invention, and the buttoning of coats an unduly tedious form of fastening, with all that snow going to waste at our very door.

When dinner-time came we had to be dragged in by the scruff of our necks. The short armistice over, the combat was resumed; but presently Charlotte and I, a little weary of contests and of missiles that ran shudderingly down inside one's clothes, forsook the trampled battlefield of the lawn and went exploring the blank virgin spaces of the white world that lay beyond. It stretched away unbroken on every side of us, this mysterious soft garment under which our familiar world had so suddenly hidden itself. Faint imprints showed where a casual bird had alighted, but of other traffic there was next to no sign; which made these strange tracks all the more puzzling.

We came across them first at the corner of the shrubbery, and pored over them long, our hands on our knees. Experienced trappers that we knew ourselves to be, it was annoying to be brought up suddenly by a beast we could not at once identify.

'Don't you know?' said Charlotte, rather scornfully. 'Thought you knew all the beasts that ever was.'

This put me on my mettle, and I hastily rattled off a string of animal names embracing both the arctic and the tropic zones, but without much real confidence.

'No,' said Charlotte, on consideration; 'they won't any of 'em quite do. Seems like something *lizardy*. Did you say a iguanodon? Might be that, p'raps. But that's not British, and we want a real British beast. *I* think it's a dragon!'

' 'Tisn't half big enough,' I objected.

'Well, all dragons must be small to begin with,' said Charlotte: 'like everything else. P'raps this is a little dragon who's got lost. A little dragon would be rather nice to have. He might scratch and spit, but he couldn't *do* anything really. Let's track him down!'

Kenneth Grahame, 'The Reluctant Dragon', 1936

[*Snow on the Pennines*]

It was, as I say, calm and clear, and the sun shone when we came out of the town of Rochdale; but when we began to mount the hills, which we did within a mile, or little more of the town, we found the wind began to rise, and the higher we went the more wind; by which I soon perceived that it had blown before, and perhaps all night upon the hills, tho' it was calm below; as we ascended higher it began to snow again, that is to say, we ascended into that part where it was snowing, and had, no doubt, been snowing all night, as we could easily see by the thickness of the snow.

It is not easy to express the consternation we were in when we came up near the top of the mountain; the wind blew exceeding hard, and blew the snow so directly in our faces, and that so thick, that it was impossible to keep our eyes open to see our way. The ground also was so covered with snow, that we could see no track, or when we were in the way, or when out; except when we were shewed it by a frightful precipice on one hand, and uneven ground on the other; even our horses discovered their uneasiness at it; and a poor spaniel dog that was my fellow traveller, and usually diverted us with giving us a mark for our gun, turn'd tail to it and cry'd.

In the middle of this difficulty, and as we began to call to one another to turn back again, not knowing what dangers might still be before us, came a surprizing clap of thunder, the first that ever I heard in a storm of snow, or, I believe, ever shall; nor did we perceive any lightning to precede the thunder, as must naturally be the case; but we supposed the thick falling of the snow might prevent our sight.

I must confess I was very much surprized at this blow; and one of our company would not be persuaded that it was thunder, but that it was some blast of a coal-pit, things which do sometimes happen in the country, where there are many coal mines. But we were all against him in that, and were fully satisfied that it was thunder, and, as we fancy'd, at last we were confirmed in it, by hearing more of it at a distance from us.

Upon this we made a full stop, and coming altogether, for we were then three in company, with two servants, we began to talk seriously of going back again to Rochdale; but just then one of our men called out to us, and said, he was upon the top of the hill, and could see over into Yorkshire, and that there was a plain way down on the other side.

Daniel Defoe, *A Tour through the Whole Island of Great Britain*, 1724

Winter brings natural inducements to jollity and conversation. Differences, we know, are never so effectually laid asleep, as by some common calamity: an enemy unites all to whom he threatens danger. The rigour of winter brings generally to the same fireside, those who moved in different directions through the other parts of the year . . .

Samuel Johnson, *The Rambler*, December 1750

Now winter nights enlarge
   The number of their hours,
And clouds their storms discharge
   Upon the airy towers.
Let now the chimneys blaze
   And cups o'erflow with wine;
Let well-tuned words amaze
   With harmony divine.
Now yellow waxen lights
   Shall wait on honey love,
While youthful revels, masques, and courtly sights
   Sleep's leaden spells remove.

This time doth well dispense
   With lover's long discourse;
Much speech hath some defence,
   Though beauty no remorse.
All do not all things well;
   Some measures comely tread,
Some knotted riddles tell,
   Some poems smoothly read.
The summer hath his joys,
   And winter his delights;
Though love and all his pleasures are but toys,
   They shorten tedious nights.

Thomas Campion (d. 1619)

[Here is] an *extract* from Sir John [Mandeville's] Journal, in which that learned and worthy knight gives an account of the freezing and thawing of several short speeches, which he made in the territories of *Nova Zembla*. I need not inform my reader, that the author of Hudibras alludes to this strange quality in that cold climate, when speaking of abstracted notions clothed in a visible shape, he adds that apt simile,

Like words congeal'd in Northern air.

Not to keep my reader any longer in suspense, the relation, put into modern language, is as follows:—

'We were separated by a storm in the latitude of *seventy-three*, insomuch, that only the ship which I was in, with a Dutch and French vessel, got safe into a creek of *Nova Zembla*. We landed, in order to refit our vessels, and store ourselves with provisions. The crew of each vessel made themselves a cabin of turf and wood, at some distance from each other, to fence themselves against the inclemencies of the weather, which was severe beyond imagination. We soon observed, that in talking to one another we lost several of our words, and could not hear one another at above two yards distance, and that, too, when we sat very near the fire. After much perplexity, I found that our words froze in the air, before they could reach the ears of the person to whom they were spoken. I was soon confirmed in this conjecture, when, upon the increase of the cold, the whole company grew dumb, or rather deaf; for every man was sensible, as we afterward found, that he spoke as well as ever; but the sounds no sooner took air than they were condensed and lost. It was now a miserable spectacle to see us nodding and gaping at one another, every man talking, and no man heard. One might observe a seaman that could hail a ship at a league's distance beckoning with his hand, straining his lungs, and tearing his throat; but all in vain—

> —Nec vox nec verba sequuntur.—OVID.
> Nor voice nor words ensued.

'We continued here three weeks in this dismal plight. At length, upon a turn of wind, the air about us began to thaw. Our cabin was immediately filled with a dry clattering sound, which I afterward found to be the crackling of consonants that broke above our heads, and were often mixed with a gentle hissing, which I imputed to the letter *s*, that occurs so frequently in the English tongue. I soon after felt a breeze of whispers rushing by my ear; for those, being of a soft and gentle substance, immediately liquified in the warm wind that blew across our cabin. These were soon followed by syllables and short words, and at length by entire sentences, that melted sooner or later, as they were more or less congealed; so that we now heard every thing that had been *spoken* during the whole three weeks that we had been *silent*, if I may use that expression. It was now very early in the morning, and yet to my surprise, I heard somebody say, "Sir John, it

161

is midnight, and time for the ship's crew to go to bed." This I knew to be the pilot's voice; and, upon recollecting myself, I concluded that he had spoken these words to me some days before, though I could not hear them until the present thaw. My reader will easily imagine how the whole crew was amazed to hear every man talking, and see no man opening his mouth. In the midst of this great surprise we were all in, we heard a volley of oaths and curses lasting for a long while, and uttered in a very hoarse voice, which I knew belonged to the boatswain, who was a very choleric fellow, and had taken this opportunity of cursing and swearing at me when he thought I could not hear him; for I had several times given him the strappado on that account, as I did not fail to repeat it for these his pious soliloquies, when I got him on ship-board.

'I must not omit the names of several beauties in Wapping, which were heard every now and then, in the midst of a long sigh that accompanied them; as, "Dear Kate!" "Pretty Mrs. Peggy!" "When shall I see my Sue again!" This betrayed several amours which had been concealed until that time, and furnished us with a great deal of mirth in our return to England.'

Joseph Addison, *The Tatler*, 1709

Happiness of evening

The winter wind with strange and fearful gust
Stirs the dark wood and in the lengthy night
Howls in the chimney top while fears mistrust
Listens the noise by the small glimmering light
Of cottage hearth where warm a circle sits
Of happy dwellers telling morts of tales
Where some long memory wakens up by fits
Laughter and fear and over all prevails
Wonder predominant—they sit and hear
The very hours to minutes and the song
Or story be the subject what it may
Is ever found too short and never long
While the uprising tempest loudly roars
And boldest hearts fear stirring out of doors

Fears ignorance their fancy only harms
Doors safely locked fear only entrance wins
While round the fire in every corner warms
Till nearest hitch away and rub their shins
And now the tempest in its plight begins
The shutters jar the woodbine on the wall
Rustles agen the panes and over all
The noisey storm to troublous fancy dins
And pity stirs the stoutest heart to call
'Who's there' as slow the door latch seemly stirred
But nothing answered so the sounds they heard
Was no benighted traveller—and they fall
To telling pleasant tales to conquor fear
And sing a merry song till bed time creepeth near

John Clare (1793–1864)

[14 December 1824]

Holborn in a fog! with the black vapour brooding over it, absolutely like fluid ink; and coaches and wains and sheep and oxen and wild people rushing on with bellowings and shrieks and thundering din, as if the earth in general were gone distracted.

No wonder Cobbett calls the place a Wen. It is a monstrous Wen! The thick smoke of it beclouds a space of thirty square miles . . .

Thomas Carlyle, *Early Letters*, vol. 2, 1886

Much difficulty was experienced in locomotion. Trains were delayed but there was no interruption of the service, for the wind being still, there was no drift. All day and night of the 17th, 18th, 19th, and 20th the snow came steadily down, and on the 21st, despite all efforts to clear it, was 27 inches deep. Traffic in the streets was now suspended, and the steamers ceased to ply, partly from want of passengers, and partly because of the dangerous obscurity. Most of the lines were blocked, and on the 22nd when the snow had an even depth of 33 inches, not a train reached London. Business was at an end. Till now the snow had been treated as a good joke by the populace who pelted each other in high spirits at their holiday, but when the trains ceased to arrive a species of desponding stupor seemed to fall upon them. The 23rd was a windy day, the breeze increasing from the east, till in the evening it blew almost a hurricane. The grains of frozen snow lifted up and driven by the wind rushed up the streets like pellets from a gun. The narrow portals of Temple Bar were impassable, so vehement was the blast, and those who attempted to get through describe the hard snow as cutting the skin of their faces in a painful manner. This gale drifted the snow in huge mounds. On the morning of the 24th the western side of Trafalgar Square was 18 feet deep in snow, the entrance to the Haymarket was blocked up, and Regent Street near the Quadrant was buried under more than 20 feet. The Thames Embankment was quite clear—the wind having an uninterrupted sweep up it—but the Houses of Parliament formed a dam across the stream of snow and against the eastern side there rose a mound at least 27 feet high. The fleet of merchantmen at the mouth of the Thames were driven on shore, and the whole northern and eastern coasts were strewn with wreckage. Many of these incidents were not ascertained till long afterwards, for the telegraph posts were blown down, the wires snapped, and all communication at an end. The bitter wind lasted five days, and is described as causing an insupportable cold which neither walls, nor curtains, nor roaring fires could overcome. It penetrated through everything. Smith says in his journal: 'We cowered round the fire, but could get no heat. We dragged our beds downstairs, and arranged them in a semi-circle round the fireplace on the carpet. Behind these we placed chairs hung with a screen of thick carpets and matting. Crouching in our beds we drew over us a heavy counterpane, and thus formed a tent indoors. Despite all this my bones felt chilled to the marrow. Etty bore it well, but my poor wife shivered incessantly, and complained that her skin was dried up and shrivelled. Emma suffered most having a weak chest, and it was clear to me that her delicate constitution would not long withstand this strain. If this was the case in our well-appointed, and even luxurious house, how dreadful must have been the sufferings of the poor. Our cellars were full of coal, and we had plenty of wine. Fortunately some friends in the country had sent us two tons of excellent potatoes as a present: and to these potatoes our ultimate preservation was due.'

On the 29th the gale moderated, but meantime snow had fallen unceasingly, and it had now reached an uniform depth of ten feet. With slight variations it continued at this depth but the drifts of course were of enormous height. The National Gallery was wholly hidden under a mound of snow. The dome of St. Paul's was alone visible, rising up like the roof of a huge Esquimoux hut. The great gilt cross on the top had been torn off by the violence of the wind. An intense frost set in, but the sky remained covered with a leaden pall of cloud, and the sun was invisible. All round the coasts there was an impenetrable wall of fog, and eight or ten icebergs are recorded to have come ashore. A berg of immense size, after beating and grinding for days against Portland breakwater, at last worked its way into the harbour, and grounded. Another got up the Solent, and two white bears swam to land from it. A third iceberg of smaller size drifted along the south coast, and after sweeping away the Brighton piers, was carried out to sea again by the tide, and lost in the fog. Not a vessel could make her port: and none dared to put out to sea, so that communication with the Continent was totally interrupted. The depth of ten feet extended over the country. Railways, canals, roads, paths, fields, all were buried to that depth, and in places the drifts rose to one-hundred-and-fifty feet. Sheep and cattle were overwhelmed and perished by thousands. Those in stalls were in a few instances kept alive for a little while by the farmers, and herdsmen cutting holes down to them. The Thames was frozen, and on the 2nd March the ice was seven feet thick off the Tower. Below Gravesend the tides carried huge blocks up and down, dashing them against each other, and against the edge of the fixed ice with a most horrible noise. During the first days of this visitation a stupor fell upon the millions of London. The upper and middle classes shut themselves up in their houses. The poorer ranks flooded the taverns in crowds, and drank in silence huddled round the fires.

Richard Jefferies, After London, 1885

London Snow

When men were all asleep the snow came flying,
In large white flakes falling on the city brown,
Stealthily and perpetually settling and loosely lying,
Hushing the latest traffic of the drowsy town;

Deadening, muffling, stifling its murmurs failing;
Lazily and incessantly floating down and down;
   Silently sifting and veiling road, roof, and railing;
Hiding difference, making unevenness even,
Into angles and crevices softly drifting and sailing.
   All night it fell, and when full inches seven
It lay in the depth of its uncompacted lightness,
The clouds blew off from a high and frosty heaven;
   And all woke earlier for the unaccustomed brightness
Of the winter dawning, the strange unheavenly glare.
The eye marvelled—marvelled at the dazzling whiteness.
   The ear harkened to the stillness of the solemn air;
No sound of wheel rumbling nor of foot falling,
And the busy morning cries came thin and spare.
   Then boys I heard, as they went to school, calling;
They gathered up the crystal manna to freeze
Their tongues with tasting, their hands with snowballing;
   Or rioted in a drift, plunging up to the knees;
Or peering up from under the white-mossed wonder,
'O look at the trees!' they cried, 'O look at the trees!'
With lessened load a few carts creak and blunder,
Following along the white deserted way,
A country company long dispersed asunder;
   When now already the sun, in pale display
Standing by Paul's high dome, spread forth below
His sparkling beams, and awoke the stir of the day.
   For now doors open, and war is waged with the snow;
And trains of sombre men, past tale of number,
Tread long brown paths, as toward their toil they go;
   But even for them awhile no cares encumber
Their minds diverted; the daily word is unspoken,
The daily thoughts of labour and sorrow slumber
At the sight of the beauty that greets them, for the charm they have
     broken.

                        Robert Bridges (1844–1930)

I got out of bed to see what had happened in the night. I was thirteen
years old. I had fallen asleep watching the snow falling through the
half-frosted windows. . . .

The world had changed. All the houses, fences, and barren trees had new shapes. Everything was round and white and unfamiliar. . . . Other snows had melted and been shovelled away, but this snow would never disappear. The sun would never shine again and the little Wisconsin town through which I plunged and tumbled to school on this dark storm-filled morning was from now on an arctic land full of danger and adventure.

When eventually, encased in snow, I arrived at the school, I found scores of white-covered figures already there. The girls had taken shelter inside, but the boys stayed in the storm. They jumped in and out of the snowdrifts and tumbled through the deep unbroken white fields in front of the school.

Muffled cries filled the street. Someone had discovered how far-away our voices sounded in the snowfall and this started the screaming. We screamed for ten minutes, delighted with the fact that our voices no longer carried and that the snowstorm had made us nearly dumb.

Tired with two hours of such plunging and rolling, I joined a number of boys who, like myself, had been busy since dawn and who now stood for the last few minutes before the school-bell with half-frozen faces staring at the heavily falling snow as if it were some game they couldn't bear to leave.

When we were finally seated in our grade-room we continued to watch the snowstorm through the windows. The morning had grown darker, as we had all hoped it would, and it was necessary to turn on the electric lights in the room. This was almost as thrilling as the pale storm still floating outside the windows.

In this yellow light the school seemed to disappear and in its place a picnic spread around us. The teachers themselves seemed to change. Their eyes kept turning toward the windows and they kept looking at us behind our desks as if we were strangers. We grew excited and even the sound of our lessons—the sentences out of geography and arithmetic books—made us tremble.

Passing through the halls during recess we whispered to one another about the snowstorm, guessing at how deep the snowdrifts must be by this time. We looked nervously at our teachers who stood in the classroom doorways stiff and far removed from our secret whispers about the snow.

I felt sorry for these teachers, particularly for the one who had taught me several years ago when I was in the Fifth Grade. I saw her as I walked by t'_e opened door of her room. She was younger than the other teachers, with two dark braids coiled around her head, a white starched blouse and soft dark eyes that had always looked kindly at me when I was younger. I saw her now sitting behind her large desk looking over the heads of her class out of the window and paying no attention to the whispers and giggles of her pupils.

As for my own teacher, a tall, thin woman with a man's face, by afternoon I had become so happy I could no longer hear what she was saying. I sat looking at the large clock over her head. My feeling on the way to school that it would never be light again and that the snowstorm would keep on for ever had increased, so that it was something I now knew rather than hoped. My eagerness to get out into the world of wind, gloom, and perpetual snow kept lifting me out of my seat.

At three o'clock we rushed into the storm. Our screams died as we reached the school entrance. What we saw silenced us. Under the dark sky the street lay piled in an unbroken bank of snow. And above it the snowfall still hung in a thick and moving cloud. Nothing was visible but snow. Everything else had disappeared. Even the sky was gone.

Ben Hecht, 'Snowfall in Childhood', 1959

A Winter Eden

A winter garden in an alder swamp,
Where conies now come out to sun and romp,
As near a paradise as it can be
And not melt snow or start a dormant tree.

It lifts existence on a plane of snow
One level higher than the earth below,
One level nearer heaven overhead,
And last year's berries shining scarlet red.

It lifts a gaunt luxuriating beast
Where he can stretch and hold his highest feast
On some wild apple tree's young tender bark,
What well may prove the year's high girdle mark.

So near to paradise all pairing ends:
Here loveless birds now flock as winter friends,
Content with bud-inspecting. They presume
To say which buds are leaf and which are bloom.

A feather-hammer gives a double knock.
This Eden day is done at two o'clock.
An hour of winter day might seem too short
To make it worth life's while to wake and sport.

Robert Frost

Indoor Games Near Newbury

In among the silver birches winding ways of tarmac wander
   And the signs to Bussock Bottom, Tussock Wood and Windy
           Brake,
Gabled lodges, tile-hung churches, catch the lights of our Lagonda
   As we drive to Wendy's party, lemon curd and Christmas cake.
     Rich the makes of motor whirring,
     Past the pine-plantation purring
       Come up, Hupmobile, Delage!
     Short the way your chauffeurs travel,
     Crunching over private gravel
       Each from out his warm garage.

Oh but Wendy, when the carpet yielded to my indoor pumps
     There you stood, your gold hair streaming,
     Handsome in the hall-light gleaming
There you looked and there you led me off into the game of clumps
     Then the new Victrola playing
     And your funny uncle saying
'Choose your partners for a fox-trot! Dance until it's tea o'clock!
     Come on, young 'uns, foot it featly!'
     Was it chance that paired us neatly,
     I, who loved you so completely,
You, who pressed me closely to you, hard against your party frock?

'Meet me when you've finished eating!' So we met and no one found
    us.
  Oh that dark and furry cupboard while the rest played hide and
    seek!
Holding hands our two hearts beating in the bedroom silence round
    us,
  Holding hands and hardly hearing sudden footstep, thud and
    shriek.
    Love that lay too deep for kissing—
    'Where is Wendy? Wendy's missing!'
      Love so pure it had to end,
    Love so strong that I was frighten'd
    When you gripped my fingers tight and
Hugging, whispered 'I'm your friend'.

Good-bye Wendy! Send the fairies, pinewood elf and larch tree
    gnome,
    Spingle-spangled stars are peeping
    At the lush Lagonda creeping
Down the winding ways of tarmac to the leaded lights of home.
    There, among the silver birches,
    All the bells of all the churches
Sounded in the bath-waste running out into the frosty air.
    Wendy speeded my undressing,
    Wendy is the sheet's caressing
    Wendy bending gives a blessing,
Holds me as I drift to dreamland, safe inside my slumberwear.

                            Sir John Betjeman

Of sheep-stealing stories I will relate one more—a case which never
came into court and was never discovered. It was related to me by a
middle-aged man, a shepherd of Warminster, who had it from his
father, a shepherd of Chitterne, one of the lonely, isolated villages on
Salisbury Plain, between the Avon and the Wylye. His father had it
from the person who committed the crime and was anxious to tell it to
some one, and knew that the shepherd was his true friend, a silent,
safe man. He was a farm-labourer, named Shergold—one of the South
Wiltshire surnames very common in the early part of last century,

which now appear to be dying out—described as a very big, powerful man, full of life and energy. He had a wife and several young children to keep, and the time was near mid-winter; Shergold was out of work, having been discharged from the farm at the end of the harvest; it was an exceptionally cold season and there was no food and no firing in the house.

One evening in late December a drover arrived at Chitterne with a flock of sheep which he was driving to Tilshead, another downland village several miles away. He was anxious to get to Tilshead that night and wanted a man to help him. Shergold was on the spot and undertook to go with him for the sum of fourpence. They set out when it was getting dark; the sheep were put on the road, the drover going before the flock and Shergold following at the tail. It was a cold, cloudy night, threatening snow, and so dark that he could hardly distinguish the dim forms of even the hindmost sheep, and by and by the temptation to steal one assailed him. For how easy it would be for him to do it! With his tremendous strength he could kill and hide a sheep very quickly without making any sound whatever to alarm the drover. He was very far ahead; Shergold could judge the distance by the sound of his voice when he uttered a call or shout from time to time, and by the barking of the dog, as he flew up and down, first on one side of the road, then on the other, to keep the flock well on it. And he thought of what a sheep would be to him and to his hungry ones at home until the temptation was too strong, and suddenly lifting his big, heavy stick he brought it down with such force on the head of a sheep as to drop it with its skull crushed, dead as a stone. Hastily picking it up he ran a few yards away, and placed it among the furze-bushes, intending to take it home on his way back, and then returned to the flock.

They arrived at Tilshead in the small hours, and after receiving his fourpence he started for home, walking rapidly and then running to be in time, but when he got back to where the sheep was lying the dawn was coming, and he knew that before he could get to Chitterne with that heavy burden on his back people would be getting up in the village and he would perhaps be seen. The only thing to do was to hide the sheep and return for it on the following night. Accordingly he carried it away a couple of hundred yards to a pit or small hollow in the down full of bramble and furze-bushes, and here he concealed it, covering it with a mass of dead bracken and herbage, and left it. That afternoon the long-threatening snow began to fall, and with snow on the ground he dared not go to recover his sheep, since his footprints would betray him; he must wait once more for the snow to melt. But the snow fell all night, and what must his feelings have been when he looked at it still falling in the morning and knew that he could have gone for the sheep with safety, since all traces would have been quickly obliterated!

Once more there was nothing to do but wait patiently for the snow to cease falling and for the thaw. But how intolerable it was; for the weather continued bitterly cold for many days, and the whole country was white. During those hungry days even that poor comfort of sleeping or dozing away the time was denied him, for the danger of discovery was ever present to his mind, and Shergold was not one of the callous men who had become indifferent to their fate; it was his first crime, and he loved his own life and his wife and children, crying to him for food. And the food for them was lying there on the down, close by, and he could not get it! Roast mutton, boiled mutton —mutton in a dozen delicious forms—the thought of it was as distressing, as maddening, as that of the peril he was in.

It was a full fortnight before the wished thaw came; then with fear and trembling he went for his sheep, only to find that it had been pulled to pieces and the flesh devoured by dogs and foxes!

W. H. Hudson, *A Shepherd's Life*, 1910

♣ He that survives a winter's day, escapes an enemy.

Carol Singers

for Deirdre

Why should it stir me, when, each face intent,
the Christmas children sing my childhood back,
clustered with hollied memories, innocent,
that lie discarded on my lonely track?

The walk in frost and darkness to the church,
doubling my steps to match my father's stride,
the greetings and the handshakes in the porch—
he held that faith, I think, until he died.

That faith, that story, half the stuff of art,
the myth, the magic of the Holy Child—
why should such sadness gather round my heart,
when every sense reports it unfulfilled,
its terms decayed, its uses out of date
as easel-painting or my classroom slate?

John Hewitt, *Out of My Time*, 1974

Even this morning, Austin, I am not in merry case, for it snows slowly and solemnly, and hardly an outdoor thing can be seen a-stirring —now and then a man goes by with a large cloak wrapped around him, and shivering at that; and now and then a stray kitten out on some urgent errand creeps through the flakes and crawls so fast as *may* crawl half frozen away. I am glad for the sake of your body that you are not here this morning, for it is a trying time for fingers and toes—for the heart's sake I would verily have you here. You know there are winter mornings when the cold without only adds to the warm within, and the more it snows and the harder it blows brighter the fires blaze, and chirps more merrily the 'cricket on the hearth.' It is hardly cheery enough for such a scene this morning, and yet methinks it would be if you were only here. The future full of sleigh-rides would chase the gloom from our minds which only deepens and darkens with every flake that falls.

Emily Dickinson, *Letters*

The sheep ran huddling together against the hurdles, blowing out thin nostrils and stamping with delicate fore-feet, their heads thrown back and a light steam rising from the crowded sheep-pen into the frosty air, as the two animals hastened by in high spirits, with much chatter and laughter. They were returning across country after a long day's outing with Otter, hunting and exploring on the wide uplands where certain streams tributary to their own river had their first small beginnings; and the shades of the short winter day were closing in on them, and they had still some distance to go. Plodding at random across the plough, they had heard the sheep and had made for them; and now, leading from the sheep-pen, they found a beaten track that made walking a lighter business, and responded, moreoever, to that

174

small inquiring something which all animals carry inside them, saying unmistakably, 'Yes, quite right; *this* leads home!'

'It looks as if we were coming to a village,' said the Mole somewhat dubiously, slackening his pace, as the track, that had in time become a path and then had developed into a lane, now handed them over to the charge of a well-metalled road. The animals did not hold with villages, and their own highways, thickly frequented as they were, took an independent course, regardless of church, post office, or public-house.

'Oh, never mind!' said the Rat. 'At this season of the year they're all safe indoors by this time, sitting round the fire; men, women, and children, dogs and cats and all. We shall slip through all right, without any bother or unpleasantness, and we can have a look at them through their windows if you like, and see what they're doing.'

The rapid nightfall of mid-December had quite beset the little village as they approached it on soft feet over a first thin fall of powdery snow. Little was visible but squares of a dusky orange-red on either side of the street, where the firelight or lamplight of each cottage overflowed through the casements into the dark world without. Most of the low latticed windows were innocent of blinds, and to the lookers-in from outside, the inmates, gathered round the tea-table, absorbed in handiwork, or talking with laughter and gesture, had each that happy grace which is the last thing the skilled actor shall capture—the natural grace which goes with perfect unconsciousness of observation. Moving at will from one theatre to another, the two spectators, so far from home themselves, had something of wistfulness in their eyes as they watched a cat being stroked, a sleepy child picked up and huddled off to bed, or a tired man stretch and knock out his pipe on the end of a smouldering log.

But it was from one little window, with its blind drawn down, a mere blank transparency on the night, that the sense of home and the little curtained world within walls—the larger stressful world of outside Nature shut out and forgotten—most pulsated. Close against the white blind hung a bird-cage, clearly silhouetted, every wire, perch, and appurtenance distinct and recognizable, even to yesterday's dull-edged lump of sugar. On the middle perch the fluffy occupant, head tucked well into feathers, seemed so near to them as to be easily stroked, had they tried; even the delicate tips of his plumped-out plumage pencilled plainly on the illuminated screen. As they looked, the sleepy little fellow stirred uneasily, woke, shook himself, and raised his head. They could see the gape of his tiny beak as he yawned in a bored sort of way, looked round, and then settled his head into his back again, while the ruffled feathers gradually subsided into perfect stillness. Then a gust of bitter wind took them in the back of the neck, a small sting of frozen sleet on the skin woke them as from a dream, and they knew their toes to be cold and their legs tired, and their own home distant a weary way.

Once beyond the village, where the cottages ceased abruptly, on either side of the road they could smell through the darkness the friendly fields again; and they braced themselves for the last long stretch, the home stretch, the stretch that we know is bound to end, some time, in the rattle of the door-latch, the sudden firelight, and the sight of familiar things greeting us as long-absent travellers from far oversea. They plodded along steadily and silently, each of them thinking his own thoughts.

Kenneth Grahame, *The Wind in the Willows*, 1908

For the people who were shovelling away on the house-tops were jovial and full of glee; calling out to one another from the parapets, and now and then exchanging a facetious snowball—better-natured missile far than many a wordy jest—laughing heartily if it went right, and not less heartily if it went wrong. The poulterers' shops were still half open, and the fruiterers' were radiant in their glory. There were great, round, pot-bellied baskets of chestnuts, shaped like the waistcoats of jolly old gentlemen, lolling at the doors, and tumbling out into the street in their apoplectic opulence. There were ruddy, brown-faced, broad-girthed Spanish onions, shining in the fatness of their growth like Spanish Friars, and winking from their shelves in wanton slyness at the girls as they went by and glanced demurely at the hung-up mistletoe. There were pears and apples, clustered high in blooming pyramids; there were bunches of grapes, made, in the shopkeepers' benevolence, to dangle from conspicuous hooks, that people's mouths might water gratis as they passed; there were piles of filberts, mossy and brown, recalling, in their fragrance, ancient walks among the woods, and pleasant shufflings ankle deep through withered leaves; there were Norfolk Biffins, squab and swarthy, setting off the yellow of the oranges and lemons, and, in the great compactness of their juicy persons, urgently entreating and beseeching to be carried home in paper bags and eaten after dinner. The very gold and silver fish, set forth among these choice fruits in a bowl, though members of a dull and stagnant-blooded race, appeared to know that there was something going on; and, to a fish, went gasping round and round their little world in slow and passionless excitement.

The grocers'! oh, the grocers'! nearly closed, with perhaps two shutters down, or one; but through those gaps such glimpses! It was not alone that the scales descending on the counter made a merry sound, or that the twine and roller parted company so briskly, or that the canisters were rattled up and down like juggling tricks, or even that the blended scents of tea and coffee were so grateful to the nose, or

even that the raisins were so plentiful and rare, the almonds so extremely white, the sticks of cinnamon so long and straight, the other spices so delicious, the candied fruits so caked and spotted with molten sugar as to make the coldest lookers-on feel faint and subsequently bilious. Nor was it that the figs were moist and pulpy, or that the French plums blushed in modest tartness from their highly-decorated boxes, or that everything was good to eat and in its Christmas dress. But the customers were all so hurried and so eager in the hopeful promise of the day, that they tumbled up against each other at the door, crashing their wicker baskets wildly, and left their purchases upon the counter, and came running back to fetch them, and committed hundreds of the like mistakes in the best humour possible; while the grocer and his people were so frank and fresh that the polished hearts with which they fastened their aprons behind might have been their own, worn outside for general inspection, and for Christmas daws to peck at if they chose.

Charles Dickens, *A Christmas Carol*, 1843

There is still something that recalls to me the enchantments of children—the anticipation of Christmas, the delight of a holiday walk—in the way the shop-fronts shine into the fog. It makes each of them seem a little world of light and warmth, and I can still waste time in looking at them with dirty Bloomsbury on one side and dirtier Soho on the other. There are winter effects, not intrinsically sweet, it would appear, which somehow, in absence, touch the chords of memory and even the fount of tears: as for instance the front of the British Museum on a black afternoon, or the portico, when the weather is vile, of one of the big square clubs in Pall Mall. I can give no adequate account of the subtle poetry of such reminiscences; it depends upon associations of which we have often lost the thread. The wide colonnade of the Museum, its symmetrical wings, the high iron fence in its granite setting, the sense of the misty halls within, where all the treasures lie—these things loom patiently through atmospheric layers which instead of making them dreary impart to them something of a cheer of red lights in a storm. I think the romance of a winter afternoon in London arises partly from the fact that, when it is not altogether smothered, the general lamplight takes this hue of hospitality. Such is the colour of the interior glow of the clubs in Pall Mall, which I positively like best when the fog loiters upon their monumental staircases.

Henry James, *Essays in London*, 1893

♣ They talk of Christmas so long that it comes.

A Christmas Poem

I see him burning in a flame
  White as a narcissus
Upon the pointed tree with silver lights
  In the jolly house.

I hear him in the bells that peal
  In the square stone tower,
And in the winter atmosphere
  He crackles like hoar.

178

You who laugh and dance in brilliance,
    And you who dream of wealth,
And you, the solemn-eyed, who grieve
    For the world's thin faith,

Come, for he comes, he who burns, rings
    In bells; he who knew well
A child's curls, and the sun-flushed rose,
    And the icicle.

Clifford Dyment, 1938

Now out of that bright white snowball of Christmas gone comes the
stocking, the stocking of stockings, that hung at the foot of the bed
with the arm of a golliwog dangling over the top and small bells
ringing in the toes. There was a company, gallant and scarlet but never
nice to taste though I always tried when very young, of belted and
busbied and musketed lead soldiers so soon to lose their heads and legs
in the wars on the kitchen table after the tea-things, the mince-pies,
and the cakes that I helped to make by stoning the raisins and eating
them, had been cleared away; and a bag of moist and many-coloured
jelly-babies and a folded flag and a false nose and a tram-conductor's
cap and a machine that punched tickets and rang a bell; never a
catapult; once, by a mistake that no one could explain, a little hatchet;
and a rubber buffalo, or it may have been a horse, with a yellow head
and haphazard legs; and a celluloid duck that made, when you pressed
it, a most unducklike noise, a mewing moo that an ambitious cat
might make who wishes to be a cow; and a painting-book in which I
could make the grass, the trees, the sea, and the animals any colour I
pleased: and still the dazzling sky-blue sheep are grazing in the red
field under a flight of rainbow-beaked and pea-green birds.

    Christmas morning was always over before you could say Jack
Frost. And look! suddenly the pudding was burning! Bang the gong
and call the fire-brigade and the book-loving firemen! Someone found
the silver three-penny-bit with a currant on it; and the someone was
always Uncle Arnold. The motto in my cracker read:

        Let's all have fun this Christmas Day,
        Let's play and sing and shout hooray!

and the grown-ups turned their eyes towards the ceiling, and Auntie Bessie, who had already been frightened, twice, by a clockwork mouse, whimpered at the sideboard and had some elderberry wine. And someone put a glass bowl full of nuts on the littered table, and my uncle said, as he said once every year: 'I've got a shoe-nut here. Fetch me a shoe-horn to open it, boy.'

And dinner was ended.

And I remember that on the afternoon of Christmas Day, when the others sat around the fire and told each other that this was nothing, no, nothing, to the great snowbound and turkey-proud yule-log-crackling hollyberry-bedizened and kissing-under-the-mistletoe Christmas when *they* were children, I would go out, school-capped and gloved and mufflered, with my bright new boots squeaking, into the white world on to the seaward hill, to call on Jim and Dan and Jack and to walk with them through the silent snowscape of our town.

Dylan Thomas, *Portrait of the Artist as a Young Dog*, 1940

There never was such a goose. Bob said he didn't believe there ever was such a goose cooked. Its tenderness and flavour, size and cheapness, were the themes of universal admiration. Eked out by apple-sauce and mashed potatoes, it was a sufficient dinner for the whole family; indeed, as Mrs. Cratchit said with great delight (surveying one small atom of a bone upon the dish), they hadn't ate it all at last! Yet every one had had enough, and the youngest Cratchits in particular, were steeped in sage and onion to the eyebrows! But now, the plates being changed by Miss Belinda, Mrs. Cratchit left the room alone

—too nervous to bear witnesses—to take the pudding up and bring it in.

Suppose it should not be done enough! Suppose it should break in turning out! Suppose somebody should have got over the wall of the back-yard, and stolen it, while they were merry with the goose—a supposition at which the two young Cratchits became livid! All sorts of horrors were supposed.

Hallo! A great deal of steam! The pudding was out of the copper. A smell like a washing-day! That was the cloth. A smell like an eating-house and a pastrycook's next door to each other, with a laundress's next door to that! That was the pudding! In half a minute Mrs. Cratchit entered—flushed, but smiling proudly—with the pudding, like a speckled cannon-ball, so hard and firm, blazing in half of half-a-quartern of ignited brandy, and bedight with Christmas holly stuck into the top.

Charles Dickens, *A Christmas Carol*, 1843

Christmas Song

The trees are all bare not a leaf to be seen
And the meadows their beauty have lost.
Now winter has come and 'tis cold for man and beast,
And the streams they are,
And the streams they are all fast bound down with frost.

'Twas down in the farmyard where the oxen feed on straw,
They send forth their breath like the steam.
Sweet Betsy the milkmaid now quickly she must go,
For flakes of ice she finds,
For flakes of ice she finds a-floating on her cream.

'Tis now all the small birds to the barn-door fly for food
And gently they rest on the spray.
A-down the plantation the hares do search for food,
And lift their footsteps sure,
Lift their footsteps sure for fear they do betray.

Now Christmas is come and our song is almost done
For we soon shall have the turn of the year.
So fill up your glasses and let your health go round,
For I wish you all,
For I wish you all a joyful New Year.

Anon.

In prolonged hard weather the freezing of a rapid stream is more than gradual; it occurs after several distinct changes. A writer of extraordinary imaginativeness like H. A. Manhood could make an imaginatively vivid word-picture of such a freezing: but the intensive sight of the mind's creative inner eye would not satisfy unless projected in parallel with what the physical sight has absorbed.

To any young genius who needs authentic material for a severe winter scene in his novel, I, an old market hack, offer gladly the following facts:

At the beginning of an ice period any stone or stick or root or fern which is sprayed or wetted near a fall or other obstruction slowly becomes coated with ice. Brambles which have pushed through the alders to find rootage for their young green tips, and have found instead the surface of the stream, become clubbed with ice. This ice, as in the case of ferns and roots, is made of innumerable layers of thin water. The club of ice on the bramble becomes slowly heavier, the bramble draws backward and forward less quickly from its spring of alder branches, until the ice extends it diagonally downstream. Water piles up against the moored ice-bottle, which loses its slender neck and becomes as though thickened by an inexperienced glass-blower. All living things feel some sort of pain; and if the weight of ice does not tear the bramble from its bush, or a thaw release it from torture, next spring it will hang there red and coarse, unbudding, until finally it withers and dies.

The frost holds. Brittle plates of ice form over still water by the sides of runs and eddies. Icicles, still called cockabells by some Devon children, hang under the falls where before water trickled very slowly. These seal the trickling places; and water trickles elsewhere, making newer cockabells. Rocks and obstacles lipped by water thicken with ice, and gradually the river level is raised. Pieces of ice break away and are carried down to the next eddy, where they lodge or ride slowly until welded into the local ice, strengthening it. . . .

The plates of ice holding frost strive to convert running water, which lags thereby and weakens in its purpose for life. Grasses and rushes help to hold the ice. Towards midday the sun in a clear sky subdues the arrogance of rime, melting first the hoof-marks of cattle and deer which wander along the banks. Above the fall the water raised by the dam of ice suddenly presses a way through. Dead leaves churn with sand in the pool below. Soon the warning sound runs down with the fuller stream: the ice cracks and whimpers, some breaking away to ride down tilting and heaving. The shadowed piers of the bridge below hold the floes, while frost instantly begins to work on them, sealing them to the stonework.

Soon the sun is behind the trees, the grass droops again as the rime settles. The weir is seen to be thicker with ice. Thin layers of water run over that ice, thickening it. If there are salmon in the pool they are scarcely stirred by the greater flow; the cold numbs them, quelling their fever to ascend for spawning.

It is very cold by the river, and now one sees passing in the water clots of semi-opaque, jelly-like substance, slightly resembling the jelly of frogs' eggs without the dark specks which are the eggs. It is like a colourless algae; but no algae grows in cold weather. The stream is filled with the slush. It is slush! Evangelical ice has conquered: the water is slowly being converted, slowly losing its joy of life, its natural brightness. The slush moves slower than the water, impeding it, striving to become static against every stone or snag, clinging to the plates of ice, which welcome it; and the running water diminishes.

At night the Dogstar is green above the south-eastern horizon: water-sounds are dulled, except where the falls roar. A mist moves over the water, becoming denser and pressing nearer the surface towards midnight. The mist of slush drags slower in the faint-hearted stream: the mist of ice-blink drags at it from the still air: only the falls roar with lessing power: and then, in one moment, the splayed glittering of the Dogstar on the water is gone. Ice lies from bank to bank.

Henry Williamson, 'The River Freezes', *Collected Nature Stories*, 1970

Blackbirds and Thrushes, particularly the former, feed in hard winters upon the shell snail horns by hunting them from the hedge bottoms and wood stulps and taking them to a stone where they brake them in a very dexterous manner. Any curious observer of nature may see in hard frosts the shells of pootys [snails] thickly littered round a stone in the lanes, and if he waits a short time he will quickly see one of these birds coming with a snailhorn in his bill which he constantly taps on the stone till it is broken. He then extracts the snail and like a true sportsman eagerly hastens to hunt them again in the hedges or woods where a frequent rustle of their little feet is heard among the dead leaves.

John Clare (1793–1864)

The fowls of heaven,
Tam'd by the cruel season, crowd around
The winnowing store, and claim the little boon
Which Providence assigns them. One alone,
The red-breast, sacred to the household gods,
Wisely regardful of th' embroiling sky,
In joyless fields and thorny thickets, leaves
His shivering mates, and pays to trusted man
His annual visit. Half afraid, he first
Against the window beats; then, brisk, alights
On the warm hearth; then, hopping o'er the floor,
Eyes all the smiling family askance,
And pecks, and starts, and wonders where he is;
Till, more familiar grown, the table crumbs
Attract his slender feet. The foodless wilds
Pour forth their brown inhabitants. The hare,
Though timorous of heart, and hard beset
By death in various forms, dark snares and dogs,
And more unpitying men, the garden seeks,
Urg'd on by fearless want. The bleating kind
Eye the bleak heaven, and next the glistening earth,
With looks of dumb despair; then, sad dispers'd,
Dig for the wither'd herb through heaps of snow.

James Thomson, from *The Seasons*, 1726–30

The Warm and the Cold

Freezing dusk is closing
　Like a slow trap of steel
On trees and roads and hills and all
　That can no longer feel.
　　　　But the carp is in its depth
　　　　　Like a planet in its heaven.
　　　　And the badger in its bedding
　　　　　Like a loaf in the oven.
　　　　And the butterfly in its mummy
　　　　　Like a viol in its case.
　　　　And the owl in its feathers
　　　　　Like a doll in its lace.

Freezing dusk has tightened
　Like a nut screwed tight
On the starry aeroplane
　Of the soaring night.
　　　　But the trout is in its hole
　　　　　Like a chuckle in a sleeper.
　　　　The hare strays down the highway
　　　　　Like a root going deeper.
　　　　The snail is dry in the outhouse
　　　　　Like a seed in a sunflower.
　　　　The owl is pale on the gatepost
　　　　　Like a clock in its tower.

Moonlight freezes the shaggy world
　Like a mammoth of ice—
The past and the future
　Are the jaws of a steel vice.
　　　　But the cod is in the tide-rip
　　　　　Like a key in a purse.
　　　　The deer are on the bare-blown hill
　　　　　Like smiles on a nurse.
　　　　The flies are behind the plaster
　　　　　Like the lost score of a jig.
　　　　Sparrows are in the ivy-clump
　　　　　Like money in a pig.

Such a frost
    The flimsy moon
        Has lost her wits.

A star falls.

The sweating farmers
    Turn in their sleep
        Like oxen on spits.

Ted Hughes, *Season Songs*, 1976

♣ It's a hard winter when one wolf eats another.

. . . the trees,—the beautiful trees! never so beautiful as to-day.
Imagine the effect of a straight and regular double avenue of oaks,
nearly a mile long, arching overhead, and closing into perspective like
the roof and columns of a cathedral, every tree and branch incrusted
with the bright and delicate congelation of hoar-frost, white and pure
as snow, delicate and defined as carved ivory. How beautiful it is, how
uniform, how various, how filling, how satiating to the eye and to the
mind—above all, how melancholy! There is a thrilling awfulness, an
intense feeling of simple power in that naked and colourless beauty,
which falls on the earth like the thoughts of death—death pure, and
glorious, and smiling,—but still death.

Mary Russell Mitford, *Our Village*, 1824–32

Janus

I am the two-headed anniversary god,
Lord of the Lupercal and the Letts diary.
I have a head for figures.

My clocks are the moon and sun,
My almanac the zodiac. The ticktock seasons,
The hushabye seas are under my thumb.

186

From All Saints to All Souls I celebrate
The *da capo* year. My emblems are albums,
The bride's mother's orchid corsage, the dark cortège.

Master of the silent passacaglia
Of the future, I observe the dancers,
But never teach them the step.

I am the birthday prescience
Who knows the obituary, the tombstone's arithmetic.
Not telling is my present.

I monitor love through its mutations
From paper to ruby. I am archivist
Of the last divorce and the first kiss.

I am director of the forgotten fiesta.
I know why men at Bacup black their faces;
Who horned at Abbots Bromley tread the mazes.

I am the future's overseer, the past's master.
See all, know all, speak not.
I am the two-faced god.

U. A. Fanthorpe, *Standing To*, 1982

The New Year

He was the one man I met up in the woods
That stormy New Year's morning; and at first sight,
Fifty yards off, I could not tell how much
Of the strange tripod was a man. His body,
Bowed horizontal, was supported equally
By legs at one end, by a rake at the other:
Thus he rested, far less like a man than
His wheel-barrow in profile was like a pig.
But when I saw it was an old man bent,
At the same moment came into my mind
The games at which boys bend thus, *High-cockolorum,*

Or *Fly-the-garter*, and *Leap-frog*. At the sound
Of footsteps he began to straighten himself;
His head rolled under his cape like a tortoise's;
He took an unlit pipe out of his mouth
Politely ere I wished him 'A Happy New Year',
And with his head cast upward sideways muttered—
So far as I could hear through the trees' roar—
'Happy New Year, and may it come fastish, too',
While I strode by and he turned to raking leaves.

Edward Thomas, 1 January 1915

New Year Exhilaration

Finds its proper weather on the 3rd day. Pressure
Climbing and the hard blue sky
Scoured by gales. The world's being
Swept clean. Twigs that can't cling
Go flying, last leaves ripped off
Bowl along roads like daring mice. Imagine
The new moon hightide sea under this
Rolling of air-weights. Exhilaration
Lashes everything. Windows flash,
White houses dazzle, fields glow red.
Seas pour in over the land, invisible maelstroms
Set the house-joints creaking. Every twig-end
Writes its circles and the earth
Is massaged with roots. The powers of hills
Hold their bright faces in the wind-shine.
The hills are being honed. The river
Thunders like a factory, its weirs
Are tremendous engines. People
Walk precariously, the whole landscape
Is imperilled, like a tarpaulin
With the wind under it. 'It nearly
Blew me up the chymbley!' And a laugh
Blows away like a hat.

Ted Hughes, from *All Around the Year*, 1979

Plough Monday was celebrated in the village in the third week of the new year, and Phillip on his last afternoon was able to see the strange procession. This rite had been held in Rookhurst, so Granmer Nye told him, ever since the walls of the first cottage had been raised from a mixture of straw, cowdung, lime, and stones. The corn being winter-sown, the last furrow usually was ploughed about the middle of January. For weeks after Christmas the patient teams of oxen plodded round the big wheatfield drawing the twin shares with their curved gleam of silver. White and agile gulls flighted from far coastal regions, joining the flocks of rooks, daws, crows, and stares. Behind the patient beasts they screamed and wheeled, the gulls graceful and soaring, alighting with gray pinions upheld on a glistening furrow suddenly to seize a worm or a beetle-case; the rooks jostling and flapping sable wings, the stares chittering and running with eagerness. Sweet chirrupings in the wake of the turmoil were made by the pied dishwashers, some of them winter visitors with slender breasts of daffodil, and all joying in the lavish gift of the ploughman guiding his team straining at the swingles.

Bill Nye the crowstarver and Samuel Caw his mate, a still smaller boy, realised their importance when the berries had been cast fanwise from the hand of Big Will'um—grains of faint gold, holding the hopes of all who toiled in the fields. The clappers sounded from the first light with the clang of the rail and the beating of tins and sometimes the hollow voices of authority floating to the desolate oddmedodds. Young rooks grew white-faced like their elders with the labour of digging into the earth. Some were shot and hung sweeing in the wind, unheeded by their greedy brethren. Now they took their tithe of the seed, since all the year they sought the wireworms and the chafergrubs that in their dark galleries and winding tunnels destroyed the rootlets.

Rookhurst rejoiced on Plough Monday. It was a half holiday, and all made merry. Even the crowstarvers left their turfed hut and clappers, and joined the revellers. They dressed Bill Nye and his mate in the skins of asses, and harnessed them to the wooden plough, a relic of olden time, that would ensure fruitfulness. Big Will'um the bailiff, tall and gaunt and heavy-booted, guided the barefooted pair. He himself took long loose strides; a boyhood in the heavy winter fields, dragging feet from the sticky clods, had given him a slouch. Every aged cottager, clad in best clothes, hobbled to his doorway to see the revel. 'Whoa, naw,' growled Big Will'um. The pair pattered to a standstill, then wheeled several times before the cottage, drawing the plough after them. The old people beamed, and dreuled their gratitude when the sacred corn-spirit had given its blessing—now the garden, soon to be sown with potatoes, cabbages, beans, onions, a lettuce or two, and a stick of rhubarb in the sun-warmed corner, would produce a fine yield, and the pig not get fever, but fatten well and perhaps reach 'dwenty-voor zgore.' From cottage to cottage they passed, making as to furrow the ground before each one. Through Rookhurst they went. George Davidson carried a blown-up pig's bladder on the end of a stick, with which he belaboured grinning labourers and the padding donkeys alike. Ribbons were wound round his body, and a red paper cap was on his head. About a hundred children, men and women, followed the procession, accompanied by dogs of all sizes and breeds. Every one was happy. Bill Nye had never felt so proud before, enwrapped as he was in the ass's skin. He knew that a big good meal was at the end of it, and, with luck, a quart of Goliath XXX.

Willie felt proud that this was his village, so impressed was Phillip, who declared that he had never heard of such a glorious idea before. Neither Jack nor his cousin was able to tell him why the asses' skins were always used by the boys who drew the lucky plough. 'It's only done in this village, having died out elsewhere,' informed Jack. 'It's an old custom too,' remarked Willie. 'At least six hundred years old.' In reality it was a survival of the rites of the corn-spirit practised since the first thought of man was to put the idea of a god into stone and food. Likewise at the harvest—to eat the firstfruits was to have within the body the power of the corn; a survival, possibly, of instinct combined with early human reasoning: the practice of eating the conquered and, therefore, possessing his strength and his cunning.

Henry Williamson, 'The Ancient Rites of the Corn Spirit'
Dandelion Days, 1930

Friday, January 24

The frost so intense last night I could scarcely keep myself alive; the water froze in the pot de chambre, although there was a good fire in my bedroom, and the jug in my wash-hand bason froze solid. I never experienced anything equal to this, excepting in the hard frost of 1788 when I was in Holland.

Winter

Sunday, January 26

The snow which had fallen in the night was so deep, I agreed to have only one Church, and that was in the evening. The boys amused themselves as well as they could.

John Skinner, *Journal of a Somerset Rector 1803–1834*

The end of the night is still, and the frost steals upon the world like moonlight from underground. No bird sings; only five or six gold-finches twitter as they flit round the heads of rigid teazels on the waste. The frost is to last, and before the sun sets the yellow menace of snow will have settled down over the earth and blotted out the Downs, which could be seen for fifty miles in the dawn. The hoar powder changes even the beauty of the familiar trees into something that never becomes a matter of course. The beeches that were yesterday a brood of giantesses are now insubstantial and as delicate as flowers of grass. The frost has been heavy, and the fields between the road and the woods are pure white without a seam. No footmark has touched the solitude, and it looks as if no one ever would cross it and enter the dark wood that is guarded so fairly. Nowhere is this inviolate look of the frosted woods more memorable than on the outskirts of London when the lamps on an open road are still glimmering and men are hurrying towards their trains. At the verge of the wood the haggard grey and drab umbelliferous plants are flowering again with crystal flowers. Inside the wood the frost has played at other mockeries. Each fragment of chalk is capped with ice, usually resembling a tooth, which is sometimes more than an inch long, and either perpendicular or slightly hooked at the tapering tip. The earth under the beeches has almost been covered by moss and ivy, and they have not been reached by the frost; yet here and there in the wood there is a gleam in those dark leaves as white as a dewy mushroom. Lying over the ivy is what might be the distaff, hastily thrown aside, from which the Fates were spinning the thread of some singularly fortunate, pure life—a distaff as it were bound round the middle with whitest wool. The distaff is a rotten peeling branch of beech, and the wool is a frost flower, such as may be found on any frosty, still day and always attached to a branch like this. The frost looks as if it had grown out of the dead wood; it is white and glossy, and curled like the under-wool which the shearer exposes on the belly of a sheep when he begins to shear it for the first

33

time; but it is finer than any wool, and the threads, as much as three inches long, are all distinct as if combed. On some branches there are more than one, and of these one may be a large handful and another no bigger than the curl of a new-born child. Often the same stick will be singled out day after day for this exquisite attention from the frost. . . .

Frost seems also to play a part in sharpening the characteristic odours of winter, such as the smell of cherry-wood or the currant bushes freshly cut by the pruner, of tar when they are dipping hop-poles, the soil newly turned and the roots exposed by the gardeners. And there is a peculiar languid sweetness in the smell of grass when the rime is melting rapidly under the sun. Above all, the fragrance of the weed-fire is never so sweet as when its bluish and white smoke heaves and trails heavily and takes wing at dawn over the frost and its crimson reflections of the flames and among the yellow tassels of the dark hedge.

Edward Thomas, *The Heart of England*, 1906

That morning's ice, no more than a brittle film, had cracked and was now floating in segments. These tapped together or, parting, left channels of dark water, down which swans in slow indignation swam. The islands stood in frozen woody brown dusk: it was now between three and four in the afternoon. A sort of breath from the clay, from the city outside the park, condensing, made the air unclear; through this, the trees round the lake soared frigidly up. Bronze cold of January bound the sky and the landscape; the sky was shut to the sun—but the swans, the rims of the ice, the pallid withdrawn Regency terraces had an unnatural burnish, as though cold were light. There is something momentous about the height of winter. Steps rang on the bridges, and along the black walks. This weather had set in; it would freeze harder tonight.

Elizabeth Bowen, *The Death of the Heart*, 1937

January 28th.—We have had rain, and snow, and frost, and rain again; four days of absolute confinement. Now it is a thaw and a flood; but our light gravelly soil, and country boots, and country hardihood, will carry us through. What a dripping, comfortless day it is! just like

the last days of November: no sun, no sky, gray or blue; one low, overhanging, dark, dismal cloud, like London smoke; Mayflower is out coursing too, and Lizzy gone to school. Never mind. Up the hill again! Walk we must. Oh what a watery world to look back upon! Thames, Kennet, Loddon—all overflowed; our famous town, inland once, turned into a sort of Venice; C. park converted into an island; and the long range of meadows from B. to W. one huge unnatural lake, with trees growing out of it. Oh what a watery world!—I will look at it no longer. I will walk on. The road is alive again. Noise is reborn. Waggons creak, horses splash, carts rattle, and pattens paddle through the dirt with more than their usual clink. The common has its old fine tints of green and brown, and its old variety of inhabitants, horses, cows, sheep, pigs, and donkeys. The ponds are unfrozen, except where some melancholy piece of melting ice floats sullenly on the water . . . The avenue is chill and dark, the hedges are dripping, the lanes knee-deep, and all nature is in a state of 'dissolution and thaw.'

Mary Russell Mitford, *Our Village*, 1824–32

Winter

Old January clad in crispy rime
Comes hirpling on and often makes a stand
The hasty snowstorm neer disturbs his time
He mends no pace but beats his dithering hand
And February like a timid maid
Smiling and sorrowing follows in his train
Huddled in cloak of mirey roads affraid
She hastens on to greet her home again
Then March the prophetess by storms inspired
Gazes in rapture on the troubled sky
And then in headlong fury madly fired
She bids the hail storm boil and hurry bye
Yet neath the blackest cloud a sunbeam flings
Its cheering promise of returning spring

John Clare (1793–1864)

Candlemas Eve

Down with the rosemary and bays,
  Down with the misletoe;
Instead of holly, now up-raise
  The greener box, for show.

The holly hitherto did sway;
  Let box now domineer,
Until the dancing Easter-day,
  Or Easter's eve appear.

Then youthful box, which now hath grace
  Your houses to renew,
Grown old, surrender must his place
  Unto the crispèd yew.

When yew is out, then birch comes in,
  And many flowers beside,
Both of a fresh and fragrant kin,
  To honour Whitsuntide.

Green rushes then, and sweetest bents,
  With cooler oaken boughs,
Come in for comely ornaments,
  To re-adorn the house.
Thus times do shift; each thing his turn does hold;
New things succeed, as former things grow old.

Robert Herrick (1591–1674)

February 1900

At Maldon (Essex). We stood on the bridge over the Blackwater at the
bottom of the town. There was snow everywhere, a very keen frost,
and a bright moon approaching the full. On either side of the river, the
wharves and warehouses were silhouetted in deep tones. The tide was
coming in, and we could hear a faint continuous crackling or mysterious rustling as the ice, constantly forming, was crunched and

crumbled gently against the projecting piles of the wharves. We stood quite still in the silent town and listened to this strange soft sound. Then we threw tiny pebbles over the bridge and they slid along the surface of the river. The water froze in broad areas as it passed under the bridge. . . . We saw a very fat and aged woman walking home, very carefully. The road was extremely slippery, and a fall would have been serious to one of her age and weight. To me she seemed rather a pathetic figure, balancing herself along. . . . And yet, if I have learnt anything, it is not to be spendthrift of pity. She would be all right.

Arnold Bennett, *Journal*, 1932

Song For February

In a dull and metric month,
A season of dank cardboard,
There is a cheery trill
Of schmaltz and egg whisks
Behind the double-glazing
Of a million spongy lounges.
Light verse is now the norm

And academic fellows
File limericks by the score.
In a brute and sallow light
Like the cheeks of an average
Punk, dead-headed roses waste
Over the pocked snow . . .
A fucked-up future snubs

The deadlands of the mullahs
Where young men dream of laws
As simple as the gallows.
And tonto in the dreck
Below the thermocline
An appetite for sex
Exhausts its fantasies.

Bored and parched, a torpid hack
Ghosts a tenth-rate life
Of President Sunsetsuma,
While Apollo pulls a string
Of ersatz novels from his lips.
The angel chimes go *ting-a-ling*
And the sugar hostess weeps

One year in four, but more and more.

Tom Paulin, The Strange Museum, 1979

The Year's Awakening

How do you know that the pilgrim track
Along the belting zodiac
Swept by the sun in his seeming rounds
Is traced by now to the Fishes' bounds
And into the Ram, when weeks of cloud
Have wrapt the sky in a clammy shroud,
And never as yet a tinct of spring
Has shown in the Earth's apparelling;
    O vespering bird, how do you know,
        How do you know?

How do you know, deep underground,
Hid in your bed from sight and sound,
Without a turn in temperature,
With weather life can scarce endure,
That light has won a fraction's strength,
And day put on some moments' length,
Whereof in merest rote will come,
Weeks hence, mild airs that do not numb;
    O crocus root, how do you know,
        How do you know?

Thomas Hardy, February 1910

I wish it were spring in the world.

Let it be spring!
Come, bubbling, surging tide of sap!
Come, rush of creation!
Come, life! surge through this mass of mortification!
Come, sweep away these exquisite, ghastly first-flowers,
which are rather last-flowers!
Come, thaw down their cool portentousness, dissolve them;
snowdrops, straight, death-veined exhalations of white and purple
    crocuses,
flowers of the penumbra, issue of corruption, nourished in
    mortification,
jets of exquisite finality;
Come, spring, make havoc of them!

I trample on the snowdrops, it gives me pleasure to tread down the
    jonquils,
to destroy the chill Lent lilies;
for I am sick of them, their faint-bloodedness,
slow-blooded, icy-fleshed, portentous.

I want the fine, kindling wine-sap of spring,
gold, and of inconceivably fine, quintessential brightness,
rare almost as beams, yet overwhelmingly potent,
strong like the greatest force of world-balancing.

This is the same that picks up the harvest of wheat
and rocks it, tons of grain, on the ripening wind;
the same that dangles the globe-shaped pleiads of fruit
temptingly in mid-air, between a playful thumb and finger;
oh, and suddenly, from out of nowhere, whirls the pear-bloom,
upon us, and apple- and almond- and apricot- and quince-blossom,
storms and cumulus clouds of all imaginable blossom
about our bewildered faces,
though we do not worship.

I wish it were spring
cunningly blowing on the fallen sparks, odds and ends of the old,
    scattered fire,
and kindling shapely little conflagrations
curious long-legged foals, and wide-eared calves, and naked
    sparrow-bubs.

I wish that spring
would start the thundering traffic of feet
new feet on the earth, beating with impatience.

                    D. H. Lawrence, from 'Craving for Spring'

March 6th.—Fine March weather: boisterous, blustering, much wind and squalls of rain; and yet the sky, where the clouds are swept away, deliciously blue, with snatches of sunshine, bright, and clear, and healthful, and the roads, in spite of the slight glittering showers, crisply dry. Altogether the day is tempting, very tempting. It will not do for the dear common, that windmill of a walk; but the close sheltered lanes at the bottom of the hill, which keep out just enough of the stormy air, and let in all the sun, will be delightful. Past our old house, and round by the winding lanes, and the workhouse, and across the lea, and so into the turnpike-road again,—that is our route for to-day. Forth we set, Mayflower and I, rejoicing in the sunshine, and still more in the wind, which gives such an intense feeling of existence, and, co-operating with brisk motion, sets our blood and our spirits in a glow.

                    Mary Russell Mitford, *Our Village*, 1824–32

All day the winter seemed to have gone. The horses' hoofs on the moist, firm road made a clear 'cuck-oo' as they rose and fell; and far off, for the first time in the year, a ploughboy, who remembered spring and knew it would come again, shouted 'Cuckoo! cuckoo!'

    A warm wind swept over the humid pastures and red sand-pits on the hills and they gleamed in a lightly muffled sun. Once more in the valleys the ruddy farmhouses and farm-buildings seemed new and fair again, and the oast-house cones stood up as prophets of spring, since the south wind had turned all their white vanes towards the north, and they felt the sea that lay—an easy journey on such a day—beyond the third or fourth wooded ridge in the south. The leaves of goosegrass, mustard, vetch, dog's mercury, were high above the dead leaves on hedge banks. Primrose and periwinkle were blossoming. Like flowers were the low ash-tree stoles where the axe had but lately cut off the tall rods; flower-like and sweet also the scent from the pits where labourers dipped the freshly peeled ash poles in tar. In the elms, sitting crosswise on a bough, sang thrush and missel thrush; in the young corn, the larks; the robins in the thorns; and in all the meadows the guttural notes of the rooks were mellowed by love and the sun.

Edward Thomas, *The Heart of England*, 1906

I, singularly moved
To love the lovely that are not beloved,
Of all the Seasons, most
Love Winter, and to trace
The sense of the Trophonian pallor on her face.
It is not death, but plenitude of peace;
And the dim cloud that does the world enfold
Hath less the characters of dark and cold
Than warmth and light asleep,
And correspondent breathing seems to keep
With the infant harvest, breathing soft below
Its eider coverlet of snow.
Nor is in field or garden anything
But, duly look'd into, contains serene
The substance of things hoped for, in the Spring,
And evidence of Summer not yet seen.
On every chance-mild day
That visits the moist shaw,
The honeysuckle, 'sdaining to be crost
In urgence of sweet life by sleet or frost,
'Voids the time's law
With still increase
Of leaflet new, and little, wandering spray;
Often, in sheltering brakes,

As one from rest disturb'd in the first hour,
Primrose or violet bewilder'd wakes,
And deems 'tis time to flower;
Though not a whisper of her voice he hear,
The buried bulb does know
The signals of the year
And hails far Summer with his lifted spear.

Coventry Patmore, from 'Winter', *Poems*, 1894

ACKNOWLEDGEMENTS

Our thanks are due to Richard Andrews, Douglas Chambers, Judith Fishman, Tim Gates, Ian Girvan, Hugh Haughton, Adam Phillips, and Sheila Southgate for their interest and encouragement.

We would also like to thank the following for permission to use copyright material in this book:

Kenneth Allsop: from *Letters to his Daughter* (Hamish Hamilton, 1974). Reprinted by permission of A. D. Peters & Co. Ltd.

W. H. Auden: extract from 'Commentary' from 'In Time of War' from *The English Auden: Poems, Essays and Dramatic Writings 1927–1939* (1977). Extract from 'Winds' from *Collected Poems* (1976). Reprinted by permission of Faber & Faber Ltd.

H. E. Bates: from *Through the Woods* (Gollancz, 1969). Reprinted by permission of the Estate of H. E. Bates and Laurence Pollinger Ltd.

Clifford Bax: 'Hot Silence' from *75 Chinese Poems: Paraphrased by Clifford Bax*. Reprinted by permission of A. D. Peters & Co. Ltd.

Samuel Beckett: from *Watt*, © John Calder (Publishers) 1976. By permission.

Sir John Betjeman: 'Harrow-on-the-Hill' and 'Indoor Games Near Newbury' from *Collected Poems* (1958). Reprinted by permission of John Murray (Publishers) Ltd.

Ronald Blythe: from *Akenfield: Portrait of an English Village* (Allen Lane, 1969). Reprinted by permission of David Higham Associates Ltd.

Elizabeth Bowen: from *The Death of the Heart* (Cape, 1937). Reprinted by permission of Curtis Brown Ltd., London, literary executors of The Estate of Elizabeth Bowen.

Malcolm Bradbury: form *The History Man* (1975). Reprinted by permission of Secker & Warburg Ltd.

George Mackay Brown: 'A Child's Calendar' and 'Weather Bestiary' from *A Calendar of Love* (1967). Reprinted by permission of the author and the Hogarth Press Ltd.

Willa Cather: from *My Ántonia* (first published 1918, new edn. Virago, 1980). Reprinted by permission of Curtis Brown Ltd.

G. K. Chesterton: from 'The Glory of Grey' from *Selected Essays* (1949). Reprinted by permission of A. P. Watt Ltd., for Miss D. E. Collins and Methuen Ltd.

John Clare: from *Selected Poems and Prose of John Clare*, edited by Eric Robinson and Geoffrey Summerfield. Copyright © Eric Robinson 1967. Reprinted by permission of Curtis Brown Ltd.

Colette: from *My Mother's House* (1953) and from *Ripening Seed*, translated by Roger Stenhouse. Reprinted by permission of Secker & Warburg Ltd.

Bob Copper: from *A Song for Every Season* (1971). Reprinted by permission of William Heinemann Ltd.

Evelyn Cox: from *The Great Drought of 1976* (Hutchinson, 1978). Reprinted by permission of A. D. Peters & Co. Ltd.

W. H. Davies: 'Frost' and 'Rich Days' from *The Complete Poems of W. H. Davies*. Reprinted by permission of the Executors of the W. H. Davies Estate and Jonathan Cape Ltd.

C. Day-Lewis: 'Now the full-throated daffodils,' from *From Feathers to Iron* from *Collected Poems*, 1954 (Hogarth Press). Reprinted by permission of Jonathan Cape Ltd., for the Executors of the Estate of C. Day-Lewis.

Paul Dehn: 'London Summer', copyright © 1965, 1976 Dehn Enterprises Ltd., from *Romantic Landscape*, first published by Hamish Hamilton Ltd. Reprinted by permission of the publisher.

Hugh de Selincourt: from *The Cricket Match* (1924). Reprinted by permission of the Executors of the Hugh de Selincourt Estate and Jonathan Cape Ltd.

Emily Dickinson: reprinted by permission of the publishers and the Trustees of Amherst College from *The Poems of Emily Dickinson*, ed. Thomas H. Johnson, Cambridge, Mass.; The Belknap Press of Harvard University Press, copyright 1951, © 1955, 1979 by the President and Fellows of Harvard College; and from *The Letters of Emily Dickinson*.

Clifford Dyment: 'A Christmas Poem' from *Collected Poems*. Reprinted by permission of J. M. Dent & Sons Ltd.

U. A. Fanthorpe: 'Janus' from *Standing To* (Harry Chambers/Peterloo Poets, 1982). Reprinted by permission of the author.

Peter Forbes: 'May' from *The Aerial Noctiluca* © Peter Forbes 1981. Reprinted by permission of Poet & Printer (Alan Tarling).

Michael Frayn: from *At Bay in Gear Street* © The Observer Ltd., 1964, 1965, 1966 and 1967. Reprinted by permission of Elaine Greene Ltd.

Robert Frost: 'A Winter Eden', 'The Cow in Apple Time' and 'After Apple-Picking' from *The Poetry of Robert Frost* (1971), edited by Edward Connery Lathem. Reprinted by permission of the Estate of Robert Frost and Jonathan Cape Ltd.

Roger Garfitt: 'Equinox' from *West of Elm* (Carcanet, 1975). Reprinted by permission of the author.

Ben Hecht: from 'Snowfall in Childhood' from *A Treasury of Ben Hecht*, © 1959 by Ben Hecht. Reprinted by permission of Crown Publishers, Inc.

John Hewitt: 'Carol Singers' and 'Suburban Spring in Warwickshire' from *Out of My Time* (1974). Reprinted by permission of John Hewitt and the Blackstaff Press.

Gerard Manley Hopkins: from *The Journals and Papers of Gerard Manley Hopkins*, edited by Humphrey House and Graham Storey, © the Society of

Jesus, 1959. Reprinted by permission of Oxford University Press on behalf of the Society of Jesus.

A. E. Housman: 'Tell me not here, it needs not saying'. Reprinted by permission of the Society of Authors as the literary representative of the Estate of A. E. Housman, and Jonathan Cape Ltd., publishers of A. E. Housman's *Collected Poems*.

Ted Hughes: 'New Year Exhilaration' by Ted Hughes, from *All Around the Year* by Michael Morpurgo & Ted Hughes (published by John Murray, 1979). 'The Warm and the Cold', 'There Came a Day', 'Swifts,' and 'Work and Play' from *Season Songs* (1976). All reprinted by permission of Faber & Faber Ltd.

Francis Kilvert: from *Kilvert's Diary* (1976), edited by William Plomer. Reprinted by permission of Mrs Sheila Hooper and Jonathan Cape Ltd.

Rudyard Kipling: from *Puck of Pook's Hill* (Macmillan, 1906). Reprinted by permission of A. P. Watt Ltd., for the National Trust and Macmillan London Ltd.

Philip Larkin: 'Cut Grass' from *High Windows* (1974). Reprinted by permission of Faber & Faber Ltd.

Laurie Lee: from *Cider With Rosie* (1959), Chapter 8. Reprinted by permission of the author and the Hogarth Press Ltd.

Norman MacCaig: 'So Many Summers' and 'Green Stain' from *A Man In My Position* (1969). Reprinted by permission of the author and the Hogarth Press Ltd.

Gordon Manley: from *Climate and the British Scene* (1952). Reprinted by permission of William Collins, Sons & Co Ltd.

A. A. Milne: extract from *Not that it Matters* published in *A Book of English Essays* (Penguin Books, 1942). Reprinted by permission of Curtis Brown Ltd., London, on behalf of the Estate of A. A. Milne.

Michael Morpurgo: from *All Around the Year* (1979). Reprinted by permission of John Murray (Publishers) Ltd.

William Morris: letter to Mrs Burne-Jones, Easter Monday, 1889 from *Letters*, edited by P. Henderson (1950). Reprinted by permission of the Society of Antiquaries of London.

Edna O'Brien: from *Mother Ireland* (Weidenfeld & Nicholson, 1976). Reprinted by permission of A. M. Heath & Co. Ltd., for the author.

Tom Paulin: 'Song for February' from *The Strange Museum*. Reprinted by permission of Faber & Faber Ltd.

Adam Phillips: 'Reading Outside', previously published in *The Honest Ulsterman*, No. 63, July/Oct. 1979. Reprinted by permission of the author.

J. B. Priestley: 'On Doing Nothing' from *Open House* (Heinemann). Reprinted by permission of A. D. Peters & Co. Ltd.

Reader's Digest: extract from *Food From Your Garden* (1977). Reprinted by permission of Reader's Digest Association Ltd.

James Reeves: extract from 'The Hour and the Storm'.

Michael Robers: 'Hymn to the Sun' from *Collected Poems*. Reprinted by permission of Faber & Faber Ltd.

V. Sackville-West: from *V. Sackville-West's Garden Book* (1968). Reprinted by permission of Michael Joseph Ltd.

George Santayana: from *Soliloquies in England* (1922). Reprinted by permission of Constable & Co. Ltd.

Septima: from Septima: *Something to Do* (Puffin Books, revised edn. 1977) pp. 136, 202, 182. Copyright © Septima Ltd., 1966. Reprinted by permission of Penguin Books Ltd.

Ellen Mary Stephenson: from *Nature Study & Rural Science* (A. & C. Black Ltd).

John Addington Symonds: from *The Letters of John Addington Symonds*, Vol. II, 1869–1884 (Wayne State University Press, 1968), edited by Herbert M. Schueller and Robert L. Peters. By permission of the editors.

Dylan Thomas: 'Holiday Memory' from *Quite Early One Morning* (Dent, 1954): extract from *Portrait of the Artist as a Young Dog* (Dent, 1940); 'We Lying by Seasand' from *Collected Poems* (Dent, 1952). Reprinted by permission of David Higham Associates Ltd.

W. J. Turner: 'Nostalgia'. Reprinted by permission of Mrs Joan F. Lisle.

Alison Uttley: from *Recipes from an Old Farmhouse* (new edn. 1973). Reprinted by permission of Faber & Faber Ltd.

Vincent van Gogh: from *The Complete Letters of Vincent van Gogh*, New York Graphic Society Books/Little, Brown & Company, Boston, 1958. All rights reserved. Reprinted by permission of Little, Brown & Company.

Richard Wilbur: 'Exeunt' from *Poems 1943–1956* (1957). Reprinted by permission of Faber & Faber Ltd.

Henry Williamson: from 'The Harmony of Nature', 'August Evening', 'The River Freezes' and *Dandelion Days*, all in *Collected Nature Stories* (1970). Reprinted by permission of Macdonald & Co. (Publishers) Ltd.

Virginia Woolf: extract from *Diary*, Vol. 3, 1925–30, edited by A. O. Bell (1980), and from *Kew Gardens* (1927). Reprinted by permission of the author's Literary Estate and the Hogarth Press Ltd.

Elinor Wylie: 'Wild Peaches' copyright 1921 by Alfred A. Knopf, Inc., and renewed 1949 by William Rose Benet. Reprinted from *Collected Poems of Elinor Wylie* by permission of the publisher.

W. B. Yeats: 'The Wheel' from *The Tower* (Macmillan, 1928). Reprinted by permission of A. P. Watt Ltd., for Michael B. Yeats, Anne Yeats and Macmillan London Ltd.

While every effort has been made to secure permission, we may have failed in a few cases to trace the copyright holder. We apologize for any apparent negligence.

INDEX OF AUTHORS

Index of Authors

Mitford, Mary Russell, 82, 154, 186, 192–4, 199
Morpurgo, Michael, 39–40, 73, 99–100, 137–8
Morris, William, 44–6

O'Brien, Edna, 2

Patmore, Coventry, 200–1
Paulin, Tom, 196–7
Phillips, Adam, 116
Priestley, J.B., 58

Reeves, James, 143
Roberts, Michael, 84–5
Rossetti, Christina, 114–15, 127
Ruskin, John, 2, 3, 23

Sackville-West, Vita, 62, 127
Santayana, George, 10–11
Selden, John, 138
Septima, 80–1, 110–11, 132
Shakespeare, William, 35, 147–8
Skinner, John, 190–1
Stephenson, E.M., 24, 68, 112–13
Stevenson, Robert Louis, 122, 146
Stubbes, Philip, 51

Symonds, John Addington, 148–9

Tennyson, Alfred, Lord, 20–1
Thomas, Dylan, 88–90, 91–2, 179–80
Thomas, Edward, 18, 41, 70–2, 94–5, 122–3, 129–30, 142–3, 153, 187–8, 191–2, 199–200
Thomson, James, 5–6, 34–5, 59, 113–14, 184
Thoreau, Henry, 24–5
Tickell, Thomas, 3
Turner, W.J., 2–3

Uttley, Alison, 93–4

Watson, Rosamund Marriott, 90–1
White, Gilbert, 26, 43, 51, 78–9, 118–19, 136–7
Whiteley, Opal, 38, 62
Wilbur, Richard, 103–4
Williamson, Henry, 96–8, 141–2, 182–3, 189–90
Woolf, Virginia, 85–6, 127
Wordsworth, William, 35–6, 153–4
Wylie, Elinor, 133–5

Yeats, W.B., 4